A Memoir

John A. Hannah in front of the new Administration Building. 1968.

A Memoir

by

John A. Hannah

Michigan State University Press   1980

Manufactured in the United States of America

Contents

My thanks are due to Russel B. Nye for invaluable editorial suggestions. Lyle Blair, Jean Busfield and Madison Kuhn also added to the end result. My thanks are also due to Leslie W. Scott and the M.S.U. Foundation for their support in the production of this volume.

INTRODUCTION

I decided to retire from the presidency of Michigan State University, in late March of 1969, to assume a post in Washington as the Administrator of the United States Agency for International Development, an independent agency of the United States government that reports to the President through the Secretary of State. The Secretary of State at that time was William Rogers, a long-time personal friend whom I had first known during the Eisenhower administration when he was Attorney General of the United States, I was Assistant Secretary of Defense for Manpower, and C. E. Wilson was Secretary of Defense.

At the time the late James Denison and the late William Combs, both long-time friends and members of the university administration, suggested that I record on tape, for later transcription, some recollections of my years spent as president of the university. I agreed to do this, with the understanding that when it was transcribed and I had had the opportunity to edit and correct it, the material would be given to the university files as part of a record that might be useful in the future for anyone interested in the history of Michigan State University.

At the time, it was assumed that this would be undertaken fairly soon. However, I found myself so heavily involved with the responsibilities of the post in Washington that I had no time to give real thought to it. I encouraged Mr. Denison and Dean Combs to refine their list of questions and forward their suggestions to me. The material furnished by Mr. Denison came in late 1972 and early 1973 and we had several conversations about it. I thought it would be better if I let time elapse to provide perspective to my recollections, and then I intended to read his outline, set aside perhaps a week or ten days or whatever, and complete the job. However, with the passage of time, this was put off for one reason and another and it was not until nearly five years later that I actually undertook recording the first installment.

For the record, I spent four and one-half years as the Administrator of the U. S. Agency for International Development and then decided to retire and return to Michigan. However, my successor in

A Memoir

A.I.D., Dan Parker, requested that, since I had played a key role in the U.S. government's participation in increasing the scope of the worldwide network of International Agricultural Research Centers, I visit each of the nine centers and provide him with a report that would serve as a guide to A.I.D. in assisting their further development.

When I returned in mid-March, 1974, after having visited all nine centers, I learned that the United States government, in response to an inquiry from the United Nations, had proposed my name as deputy to the Secretary-General of the World Food Conference, planned for November of 1974. I made a trip or two to New York and visited with Kurt Waldheim, Secretary-General of the U.N., and others, and later with Sayed Marei, the distinguished Egyptian Minister of Agriculture, who was Secretary-General of the World Food Conference.

I agreed to accept that responsibility. When the World Food Conference was about to start in Rome in early November of 1974, Mr. Marei informed me that he was soon to be elected President of the Peoples Assembly in Egypt, but that he would stay with the conference until it was completed and then return to Cairo. He suggested to the U. N. Secretary-General that I wind up the work of the conference. Subsequently, Mr. Waldheim asked me to do that.

One of the recommendations of the World Food Conference was that a new international organization to be known as the United Nations World Food Council be established. Secretary-General Waldheim asked me to remain for a few weeks to get that work started and to give him time to find an executive director to head the secretariat of the World Food Council. The few weeks turned into many, and I ended up as the executive director with the understanding that I would stay only through the first meeting of the council in June, 1975. Later that was extended to the second meeting of the council in June, 1976, and now as I dictate this we are preparing for the third meeting of the World Food Council in June, 1977.

As I make this first recording on Monday, January 17, 1977, in my office at my farm in Dansville, I recognize that memories are fallible. I never kept a diary. I have had neither the time nor the inclination to review materials in the university files dealing with the period of my presidency. I shall follow the outline of the questions prepared by James Denison and William Combs, dealing with the events of those years as I remember them, reminding the reader that this is a memoir, not a history.

PART I
THE EARLY YEARS

Please tell us something of your family background, including the business activities in which your father was engaged and in which you and your brothers participated. A brief statement of your educational experiences would be helpful. For example, tell us what high school you attended, your junior college experience, your transfer to the University of Michigan (with a law career in mind) and your transfer to M.A.C.

I was born October 9, 1902, in a small home on Linden Avenue just north of Burton Street in Grand Rapids, across the road from the family-owned market garden and greenhouses operated by my grandfather Alfred Hannah and his two sons, my father Wilfred Steele Hannah and his brother George A. Hannah.

My grandfather Alfred was born in England of Scottish parentage. His parents had moved from Ayr in Scotland to Welny, a suburb of Cambridge in England. His father died and left his widow with several young children. When he was seventeen years old he migrated from England to the United States, all alone. A sister, Mrs. Carolyn Patterson, had preceded him. I remember early family conversations about Aunt Carolyn but I have no recollection of ever having seen her and we have lost track of her family.

My grandfather came to the little town of Augusta in Kalamazoo County, where he was first employed as a blacksmith. He was strong physically, but short in stature, about five feet six inches tall—probably due to faulty nutrition in his youth. He met my grandmother, Jane Orell Steele, in Augusta, where she was a schoolteacher. They were married in Schoolcraft in 1876 and moved to Grand Rapids.

My grandmother Hannah had come to Michigan from Honeoye, a small town in western New York State near Livonia, where she had been well educated for that time. She graduated from what was then called a female seminary, later a state teacher's college. As a result of her work as a teacher, she had accumulated some savings. After she and my grandfather were married, they acquired a few acres of land on Eastern Avenue Road south of Burton Road, and my grandfather became involved in the market gardening business. He later branched into the florist business and built, owned, and operated extensive greenhouses on Eastern Avenue north of Burton Street. He operated a retail flower store in downtown Grand Rapids on Monroe Street near Fulton Street Park, across from the Grand Rapids Press Building and adjacent to the old Danne and Witters Grocery. I remember very well that my grandfather visited the downtown flower store practically every day, and he always spent Saturday evening there reviewing the week's work and finances.

The market gardening business on Eastern Avenue Road included the land north of Burton Street operated by my grandfather and his younger son, George, as well as the original family home of grandfather and grandmother, south of Burton Street on Eastern Avenue, then owned by my father. The market garden business involved a daily trip to the wholesale market of Grand Rapids, very early every morning during the growing season, by either my grandfather or my father. In the early days this trip started about 3:00 A.M. with a horsedrawn vehicle, to be there at 4:00 A.M. when the market opened. After the sales were completed the products were delivered to the various grocers or wholesalers. It was a real treat to be permitted occasionally to accompany them on this trip.

My father did not attend a primary school. My grandmother felt that she could give him a better primary education at home than that provided by the one-room country schools of the day. She was a scholarly person, able to read and translate rapidly from Latin and Greek, the academic languages for scholars of her youth.

My father was graduated from the Grand Rapids High School, now known as Grand Rapids Central High, played on the football team and incurred a serious injury to one of his legs. Many years later this developed into osteomyelitis, which required a series of operations and eventually the hollowing out of the main bone of one leg from the knee to the ankle and the removal of the bone marrow. I remember very well that one could lay a broomstick in the healed scar in the front of his leg.

On completion of high school there was some discussion about my father's going to college, but it was decided that it would be advisable for him to go into the florist business with my grandfather. My father had become very much interested in horticulture and was generally regarded as quite an authority on scientific agriculture. I remember the many large and impressive looking books in his library that dealt with botany and horticulture. He always referred to plants by their scientific names.

Later in his life he was active in the local school affairs. At that time we were living in a rural school district, Paris Township, District No. I, which had a three room school, a pretty good sized rural school then. For many years he was the director of the school board and had a good deal to do with the operation of the school. He was also one of the founders of the old Grand Rapids Growers Association, a cooperative marketing organization for greenhouse and vegetable growers. For much of the time he was president or chairman of that organization.

My mother, Mary Ellen Malone, was born and raised in Grattan Township of Kent County, about twenty miles northeast of Grand Rapids in the community of Parnell, which had a store, a blacksmith shop, St. Patrick's Catholic Church, and a church school. The store and the blacksmith shop had been sold off my grandfather's farm. The Catholic church installations were on the other side of the road. My mother's father was John M. Malone. I think he had only a grade school education, but he was regarded by the farmers around as an authority on livestock and livestock diseases and, since there were no veterinarians in the area, he was generally referred to as "Doc" Malone. His family had migrated from Ireland when he was a small boy and his brothers and sisters lived in or about Grand Rapids, except for his older sister, Mrs. Mary Feeley, who lived in Champion, Michigan, up in the Copper Country of the Upper Peninsula.

My mother's mother was born Julia Ann Laughlin, whose parents had come from Ireland and were farmers in Grattan Township. After my mother had finished the local schools, she went to Ferris Institute, the predecessor of the present Ferris State College. She knew and had a high regard for Woodbridge N. Ferris, the proprietor of Ferris Institute, who was later Governor of Michigan and still later United States Senator from Michigan. She earned a teacher's certificate and taught in the grade schools of Kent County for a few years until she married my father.

My mother and father were practically the same age. His birthday was on February 14, Valentine's Day, 1879, and her birthday was on January 29, 1879. After they were married, they lived in a house on Linden Avenue, adjacent to the gardens and greenhouses of the Grand Rapids Floral Company, which was the firm name of my grandfather's business in those days. Later, a new house was built for them on Eastern Avenue. After my grandmother Hannah's death, my grandfather moved into that house and our family moved into the old residence that had been built by my grandfather and grandmother many years earlier. This was and is a large colonial type house, just south of Burton Street, on the west side of Eastern Avenue. The house still stands there, although it has now been turned into three or four apartments and there are three large apartment buildings west of it where my father's greenhouses used to be. The original market garden was subdivided into city lots for houses many years ago.

In my own family, there were four children. I was the oldest, next was my brother, Arthur Joseph Hannah, and then my sister Julia, who later married Vincent Vandenburg. The youngest was W. Harold Hannah. Arthur graduated from Michigan State in 1927 in Landscape Architecture, and Harold in Poultry Husbandry in 1932. Julia was a student at M.S.C. when my father's health failed and she returned to Grand Rapids to assist my mother. Harold remained out of college for a year to work in the family business and Arthur resigned his work in Chicago and returned to Grand Rapids, eventually to take over management of the poultry business. Harold later took over management of the floral business.

My father turned the responsibility for the poultry flock over to me when I was five or six years old. The chickens became my total responsibility. At that time, they were Barred Plymouth Rocks. I later became interested in other breeds and my father bought me two or three settings of Black Orpington eggs. Very early I began to exhibit chickens at the poultry shows around the state, of which there were several at that time, and at the State Fair in Detroit. I made my first trip to Chicago alone by train when I was about thirteen to exhibit Black Orpingtons at the poultry show in the Coliseum.

Chickens soon became a fairly substantial business. There were many fanciers at that time who exhibited poultry. Chickens produced for eggs or meat were incidental to the fanciers. Emphasis was all on types, colors and color patterns, breed characteristics, etc.

Dudley Waters, head of one of the large banks in Grand Rapids, had a gentleman's farm north of Grand Rapids and annually exhibited his Holstein cattle in the farmers' fairs of Michigan and nearby states. He became interested in Black Orpington chickens and in me and purchased some of them from me. It was that fact that made it possible years later for me to go to college.

Now, about my early education. For the first three grades I attended the Oakdale primary school in Grand Rapids. When my parents moved to my grandmother's earlier home, we transferred to Paris District No. 1 for the next five grades. After eighth grade, all students took the country-wide examinations and those who were successful received a certificate and participated in county graduation exercises.

I then proceeded to Grand Rapids South High School and was one of the first students to register in it. I remember standing second or third in line to register the day that South High School first opened. That was in the fall of 1915. My birthday was on the ninth of October. I was twelve years old when I registered as a ninth grade student at South. I graduated four years later, in the spring of 1919, at the age of sixteen. The school was several miles from the home on Eastern Avenue Road. In those days there were no school buses or anything of that sort; when the roads were clear I rode a bicycle to school or when they were muddy or snow covered I walked.

There were several excellent teachers in Grand Rapids South High School—certainly some of them succeeded in interesting me in many things. I recall particularly a Miss Sweitzer who taught chemistry. I was not especially interested in chemistry, but she was interested in me. Mary Newel Eaton, who taught English, was a fine teacher and I recall carrying on conversations with her over a period of many years. Mary L. Mueller was a first-rate teacher of science who got me interested in botany, biology, and birds. I learned the names of all the wild animals, all the birds, and all the flowers that one could find walking in the open spaces, in the woods, or along the creeks which were then readily available. An excellent teacher of German, Fraulein Heidt, widened my interest in other countries and people. Arthur Krause, who later became principal of South High and then Superintendent of the Grand Rapids schools, and P. L. Churm I also remember as very effective teachers and I continued to keep in touch with them over many years.

As a result of their influence—possibly aided by the early influence of my grandmother Hannah and my father's interest in education and everything else—there had been a family decision that I ought to go to school beyond high school. After the death of my grandmother Hannah, my grandfather had remarried and his second wife and her family had taken over that household, so the relationship was not as close as it had been. In any event, my grandfather Hannah indicated that he would make an effort to see to it that I had the chance to go to college. In his view, agriculture was not very important and he hoped that I might become a lawyer.

During the time I was in high school, I continued in the poultry business and became the secretary of the West Michigan Poultry Association and eventually of the State Poultry Association, as well as superintendent of the poultry department at the West Michigan State Fair in Grand Rapids and later at the Michigan State Fair in Detroit. I had also developed an interest in studying scientific agriculture, but since the family had no great enthusiasm for that, I decided that I would start down the road toward becoming a lawyer. Due to the strained relationships within the Hannah family, it was clear that money for college would not be easily come by. My father had four children to educate and financing the family was a nip and tuck operation, although I do not think I realized it at that time.

The Grand Rapids Junior College was one of the first junior colleges in the country. It functioned on the fourth floor of Grand Rapids Central High School. In the fall of 1919, having completed South High School, I enrolled in Grand Rapids Junior College and attended it for two years. Here again, there were some excellent teachers. Burton Smith made me understand and enjoy physics. Miss Bailey, a teacher of botany, was another excellent teacher. The Hinsdale sisters, Mary and Mildred, one who taught history and the other political science, whetted my appetite for high quality education. Mr. Andrews, Mr. Wilcox, and others stimulated in me a desire to make of myself the best person possible—considering the raw material.

During the time I was enrolled in Grand Rapids Junior College, my grandfather Hannah died and the possibility of his financial aid ceased to exist. My parents wanted to do and did all they could to help me financially every step of the way. To help myself, I went to see Dudley Waters, the banker I referred to earlier, to inquire whether or not he would be interested in loaning me some money so that I might enroll in the University of Michigan Law School. At that time, if one's grades were satisfactory, it was possible after two years in the literary college at Ann Arbor (in my case the Grand Rapids Junior College record was acceptable) to go directly into law school, so that after three years of law school or a total of five years of undergraduate education, one could graduate with a law degree.

Dudley Waters loaned me $900 for the first year, 1921-22. To me that was a very large sum of money and I was bothered from the beginning with the knowledge that it would have to be paid back. In those days, one went from Grand Rapids to Ann Arbor by train and the first trip was quite an event. I rented a room at 1130 West Washtenaw, a site now occupied by the University of Michigan Medical School. It was a typical student rooming house. There were three or four of us from Grand Rapids living there. Frank M. Townsend, who later became a medical doctor in Grand Rapids; Erwin Stegmier, a student in engineering of whom I have lost track; and one or two others.

One of the good friends that I made in the freshman law class at Ann Arbor was Jerome Dunne, whose father had been governor of Illinois. He was on the University of Michigan football team, and I think it was my acquaintance with him that first got me seriously interested in collegiate athletics. I was a tall, scrawny youngster, something over six feet tall and about 141 pounds at the time that I started as a law student at Ann Arbor. So while I might have been interested in athletics, I certainly was not an athlete. The excitement in Ann Arbor for the Ohio State-Michigan football game that first fall involved me with all the enthusiasm of the average college student of that era. I have forgotten whether Michigan or Ohio won.

As my first year in law school progressed, I soon realized that I was going to have to borrow more money if I was going to continue studying law. I was interested in what happened to graduates of the Michigan law school. Most of them at that time, after passing their state bar examinations, hung up their shingles and started private practice. It seemed to me that unless a young man had a relative who was in a well-established law firm, getting started in the legal business was going to be difficult.

I remember studying the Grand Rapids telephone directory and looking over the list of the local lawyers; I was impressed with the large number of them and by the few I had ever heard of. It was clear to me that if I returned to Grand Rapids to be a lawyer and started on my own, it was going to be a tough pull, as contrasted to someone like "Duke" Dunne who would go directly into the family law firm in Chicago.

In the winter of 1921–22, E. C. Foreman, who had been on the Agricultural Extension staff at M.A.C. and was head of the Poultry Department, came to visit me in Ann Arbor. I was still secretary of the Michigan State Poultry Association. He asked me what I was going to do when I finished law school and I told him frankly I did not know. Before the conversation was over, he suggested that if I came to East Lansing and took a degree in agriculture, he would give me a job as an extension poultryman at an annual salary of $2,500. Two thousand five hundred dollars a year sounded to me like a tremendous amount of money.

I thought about it and talked it over with my father. He really wanted me to stay in Ann Arbor, but he felt that his children should decide what they were going to do with their lives, and that if I wanted to embark on a different trail it would be all right with him.

I remember going to see Charles W. Garfield, president of the Grand Rapids Savings Bank, to ask his advice. A friend of my grandfather and grandmother Hannah, Mr. Garfield was an alumnus of M.A.C. and former member of the State Board of Agriculture, then the board of control for M.A.C. His advice was that I ought to do whatever I wanted to do. He thought agriculture was an honorable profession. That was what I wanted to hear—one tends to like those with whom he agrees or who agree with him.

So I decided that I would make a trip to East Lansing and talk to people in the College of Agriculture to see whether or not I would be acceptable as a student, and to find out what would be required to qualify for a Bachelor's degree in agriculture. At that time, all of the academic buildings on the East Lansing campus were on the north side of the Red Cedar River. The Agriculture Building was the building that is still known as the College of Agriculture. The old Library was in the building that was later the Administration Building where I occupied an office for something over thirty-four years as Secretary and President.

I remember very well going into the office of the Dean of Agriculture, Robert S. Shaw, later to become President of Michigan State. His assistant was Elton B. Hill, who became Head of the Department of Farm Management and still resides in East Lansing.

They reviewed my record from Grand Rapids Junior College and from the law school at the University of Michigan and decided to accept me. I would be held for all the required courses in agriculture, but I could either take them in class or, if I could convince the professors or heads of the departments that I had the competence, I could pass some of them by examination. It was possible then, with the permission of the department chairman, to take an examination at the beginning of any term; if one passed it he could get full credit in the course. Hill and others thought that it would be difficult to complete the requirements within a single year, but I could try if I wanted to.

As a result, in the fall of 1922 I came to East Lansing as a transfer student in the College of Agriculture, having taken no courses in agriculture before that time. To make a long story short, I did pass off many of the required courses, took classes in those I did not think I could pass by examination, and completed my requirements so that in June of 1923 I graduated with the class of 1923, having been a member of it for only one year. I went to work immediately for the Poultry Department at the salary of $2,500 a year. The commencement exercises were about June 20 on the second floor of what is now the Women's Physical Education Building, and the following week I went out into the field as an extension poultryman.

I remember very well that the first farm group I talked to was in Newaygo, having gone from Lansing to Grand Rapids and Grand Rapids to Newaygo by train. This was my first assignment to speak to a farmers' club and I was very nervous about it. It seems to me that after that I never got up to speak without feeling weak in the legs. I had taken no courses in public speaking, and for the first, and many years after, all my speeches were ad libbed.

Later, when I became President of Michigan State and listened to some of my speeches that had been recorded, I learned that what I actually said and what I thought I had said or planned to say were often quite different. I then accepted the advice of more experienced university presidents who told me that an administrator should never speak publicly except from a written script so that he could deal with his critics afterwards on the basis of what he *knew* he had said rather than on what he *thought* he had said.

Please tell us about your early involvement in the hatchery business.

After I became an extension poultryman, I suggested to my father that he should put increasing emphasis on the egg production and breeding stock part of the poultry business. He built a new poultry house and I purchased for him 1000 White Leghorn baby chicks from W. C. Eckard, the County Agricultural Agent for Van Buren County in Paw Paw, who had one of the first flocks of Tancred strain White Leghorns in the middle west. Douglas Tancred, a poultry breeder in the state of Washington, had produced a strain of White Leghorns that consistently laid many more eggs than any other strain of chickens up to that time.

From that beginning, poultry at the Grand Rapids family farm became a real business. My father, joined by my brother Arthur and later by my younger brother Harold, emphasized scientific poultry breeding and later added a commercial chick hatchery business. They were interested in trapnesting all the layers and in pedigree breeding all of the chicks, and were also involved from the beginning in the record of performance, or for short, the R.O.P. Program. They soon became successful egg production breeders and acquired a substantial national reputation as such.

It may not sound modest, but I had something to do with convincing the poultry breeders of America that they should develop a semi-official system for authenticating poultry records, thus making it possible to differentiate between breeders who were scientific and bred with real quality, and those who only claimed quality.

Out of this effort there developed a national poultry breeding plan and a national system of state R.O.P. associations, sponsored in part by the land grant colleges throughout the country. From this too came a series of official egg laying contests, also sponsored by the land grant colleges. There was then a large poultry industry in Holland, Zeeland and much of Ottawa County, Michigan. A substantial fraction of the commercial hatchery business of the United States was located there for many years. All of this received national recognition from the poultry industry.

I was elected president of the International Baby Chick Association, which became a leader in sponsoring honest advertising and in trying to weed out poultrymen who had not been too scrupulous in their operations. Many interesting ramifications developed as a result of that effort by the I.B.C.A., not the least of which was the fact that at an annual convention held in Milwaukee, one of the larger hatcherymen of the country who had been found somewhat less than honest in his operations, appeared before the board of directors to defend himself. After he lost his case, he pulled a pistol out of his pocket and shot and killed the president of the association, Charles Sawyer of Ohio; shot the secretary, Reese Hicks of Kansas City; sent a bullet over the heads of some of the rest of us; put the gun to his own head, pulled the trigger, and fell dead at my feet. This occurred in the public auditorium in Milwaukee.

I assume that the presidency of the I.B.C.A. had something to do with the fact that I was offered the opportunity in 1932 by General Hugh Johnson's National Recovery Administration to take over the leadership of the Poultry Hatchery Code. After Michigan State College granted my request for a leave of absence for a year (which was later extended), I left East Lansing to become the managing director of the Poultry Industry Hatchery Breeder Code, with headquarters in Kansas City. In this post, I traveled all over the United States, organized hatchery breeder groups in all states of the union, and found myself the "Czar" of an important national industry. As a relatively young man, I was responsible for deciding whether or not a business could continue in business. All firms were required to belong to the organization, pay fees, subscribe to the principles adopted by the industry, and be subject to examination with reference to ethics, integrity, etc. We had a national board of advisors, but actually I more or less called the tune.

After a year with the hatchery code I became concerned that there was something wrong with the system. It did not seem to me that it was appropriate for a young fellow who knew no more than I did to have the authority to establish the course and pattern of an entire industry, or to determine whether individual poultrymen or hatchery operations could stay in business or be forced out of it. My leave for the first year from June, 1932 to June, 1933 had been extended by the college for another year if I wanted it, but in the fall of 1933, I had about decided that I did not want to follow that role as a longtime career. One of the big Chicago packers asked if I would be interested in giving up the job in Kansas City to go to Chicago to head up their produce department or that part of it that had to do with poultry, eggs, and butter. It meant three times as much salary as I was getting.

This required me to take a hard look at what I wanted to do with my life. If I wanted to make money, here was a good opportunity. But I had become pretty well sold on the work of the Cooperative Extension Service and had a large number of friends all over Michigan. For ten years I had spent an average of 200 days a year in the field in Michigan as Extension Poultryman, and I felt, with some justification, that there were few places in the state where I was more than a few miles away from someone I knew as a friend. I spent two months each year in the Upper Peninsula, one month in the winter and one month in the summer, and traveled the entire state. I was much impressed with what could be done to improve the lives of farm people. It seemed to me then that M.S.C. could make a significant contribution to the improvement of the lives of not only rural people, but of all people.

Later, in the late summer of 1934, President Shaw invited me to meet him in Chicago. He wanted to talk about my returning to Michigan State to do something else, and I agreed to meet him there on the occasion of one of the early National All Star high school football games.

Dr. Shaw wanted to talk to me about returning to Michigan State to replace Herman Halladay, who was retiring as Secretary of the

Board of Agriculture after a good many years of service in that capacity. At that time, the secretary's office was on the ground floor of the old Library (later known as the old Administration Building) while the president's office was on the second floor of the new Library —the building now occupied by the Museum.

The secretary's office was a peculiar kind of entity. It had evolved as a result of some pretty strong men who preceded me as Secretary of the Board of Agriculture. Secretaries of the board played a powerful role in the day-to-day administration of the physical plant, in dealings with state government and the state legislature, and in the institution's business operations. With the college only three miles from the state capitol, it was easily subject to scrutiny by officials of the state government, the legislature, and individual legislators themselves.

When President Shaw asked me if I would accept the job, I told him I was interested, but I would have to first be released from my current responsibility. He offered me a salary of $4,200 per year which was much less than what I was receiving from N.R.A., and about one-fifth of what I would have received had I taken the job with the Chicago packing firm.

I had already concluded that there were things more important to me than making money and I had about made up my mind that I would rather return to a university—particularly to Michigan State College—than do anything else. It seemed to me that when a person gets old and looks back over his life, what is important in it is not prestige or the amount of money in the bank, but rather whether or not he feels that his life has been useful. If he has been able to contribute, even in some small way, to making it possible for people to live lives that are more satisfying to them than they might otherwise have been, that, it seems to me, is probably the most meaningful of all life's satisfactions. So I decided to return to East Lansing, January 1, 1935 as the Secretary of the College and Secretary of the State Board of Agriculture.

Upon my arrival, President Shaw gave me three specific assignments for immediate attention. The order in which I list them is not necessarily his order of relative importance, but the order of my difficulty in carrying them out. The first had to do with the Michigan

State College bonds that were held by the State Treasury in the State Highway Sinking Funds Account. The money had been borrowed many years earlier by the college to build the Union Memorial Building and to provide the funds for the construction of the football stadium. The interest on these bonds had not been paid for several years. They were in default, and in its current session, the legislature raised the question of how the state was to collect its money from the college. Perhaps this money, it was suggested, should be deducted from the legislative appropriations made for college operations. President Shaw wanted me to see if something could be done to have these bonds canceled or to get the legislature to make appropriations to cover the debt; or, he hoped, to provide additional funds to complete the Union Building, which still remained unfinished.

Another matter that concerned him was the total amount of legislative appropriations customarily received for the operation of the college. At that time the amount appropriated for the annual budget had been reduced substantially from earlier levels to one million, one hundred and seventy-eight thousand dollars ($1,178,000). One million dollars of this was for the operation of the college and one hundred and seventy-eight thousand dollars was apportioned to the Cooperative Agricultural Extension Service. Salaries of professors and wages for all other employees had actually been reduced because of the college's low income. Competition in the legislature for appropriations was tough. President Shaw wanted me to give my best efforts to dealing with the legislature and with state government, so that the college received sufficient funds to improve its quality and increase its enrollment.

The third item that bothered the President, although of less importance, was the old Farm Lane bridge that connected the college proper with the college farm. The bridge was in a sad state of disrepair, already condemned by the state as unsafe. Nothing had been done about it, since questions were always being raised as to whether or not it should be closed as a public road. He hoped that something could be done to settle the problem quickly.

I learned later that when Mr. Shaw recommended to the State Board of Agriculture that I be employed as the new secretary, a question had been raised by a board member who thought that the proposed stipend was a "pretty fancy salary" for a young man of my age, but I knew nothing about that until later. So I moved into the secretary's office on the south side of the first floor of the old library building at the beginning of January, 1935.

I inherited Marie Mercier from Herman Halladay as my secretary. She was and is a remarkable woman, competent, efficient and always pleasant to everybody. She added great strength to the office and to Michigan State. Miss Mercier was my secretary all the time I was in the secretary's office and continued as secretary for Karl McDonel when he succeeded me. When I later moved upstairs to the president's office, Ruth Jameyson had been Mr. Shaw's secretary for some years, and she continued to serve with me during the years that I was president, almost twenty-eight years. Both of these women were remarkably effective in their posts, wholly loyal to the university and smart enough to never talk about university business outside of the office.

> *Your first public employment was in the extension service.*
> *What kind of work did you do, and for how long? Certainly*
> *you developed contacts with farm and community leaders*
> *who would be helpful in your later career. Will you discuss*
> *them, please? Was it at this period that you developed your*
> *lasting interest in travel, both in the U.S. and the world?*

During my ten years in the extension service, as I worked with others elsewhere in the country, I became convinced of the need for additional scientific research in increasing the capacity of hens to lay eggs, and in finding ways by which chickens and turkeys might convert grains or feed into poultry meat more efficiently. The results of modern researchers in genetics were first used intelligently by poultry departments at Michigan State and other land grant colleges. It resulted eventually in taking the chickens off the farms and placing them into factory-like operations with almost complete automation.

Michigan State also played a part in the internationalization of poultry information, and in the spread of scientific knowledge from one country to another. From this beginning, what had originally been the American Poultry Science Association evolved into the World Poultry Science Association, which included practically all university poultry scientists in North America and Western Europe and eventually the world. This organization sponsored a series of World Poultry Congresses, in which I participated.

The first ones were in Ottawa, Canada, in 1927, and in London in 1930. I think the next was in Copenhagen in 1933, then in Berlin in 1936 and Cleveland in 1939, just prior to the outbreak of World War II in Europe. I remember very well coming back from the World Poultry Congress in Berlin, where I had been the chairman of the American delegation and had seen and met Adolph Hitler. I remember making speeches, when I returned, suggesting the possibility of war, based on what we had seen of highways being built connecting all the principal cities of Germany to the borders, the camouflaged military trains, and the evidence of military activities everywhere.

As a result of my involvement in the world poultry congresses and of what happened in World War II, I came to believe that not much of lasting importance is likely to be settled on battlefields. The only real hope for the human race, I am convinced, is to find a way for the peoples of all colors, all races, and all religions to agree, not necessarily on politics or economic philosophies, but on how to get on with peaceful efforts at solving the most important basic human problems. I shall return to this subject when I deal with developments at Michigan State during and after World War II.

What motivated you to return to Michigan State? Will you recall your experiences in the secretary's office, and give an appraisal of the situation of the college at that time? What did you then envisage as the prospects for the college to develop into a true university and national leader?

I have already described the assignments given to me by President Shaw when I returned to the college as secretary. We went immediately to work. We decided at the outset that Michigan State should never become involved in partisan politics. A respectable public educational institution must provide the same kinds of service to Democrats, Republicans, and people of any other political persuasion. It must deal equally and even-handedly with members of the legislature and with personnel in the governor's office as well as in the other state offices.

At the beginning of my tenure as secretary, M.S.C. was a typical land grant, A. & M.-type college. As land grant colleges developed over the latter half of the nineteenth century, and the early twentieth, the forty-eight states divided down the middle; twenty-four of the states had a single unified university while in the other twenty-four there were separate state universities and so-called A. & M. (agriculture and mechanical engineering) colleges offering agriculture, mechanical arts (later called engineering), home economics, veterinary medicine and the rest.

As M.S.C. grew in size and influence, it became clear that the institution could not turn out top quality farmers, engineers or home economists unless they were well grounded in the basic sciences, with a general knowledge of history, the arts, and of other components of a sound education. The college needed to become a much better institution, educationally, than it had been, with wider horizons and broader objectives. When it provided students on its campus with education in the sciences and the arts, that education must be of the best quality. When its graduates went out into the world they had to compete on equal terms with graduates of the best of the nation's other public universities, such as Michigan, Wisconsin, Illinois, Ohio State, Minnesota, or California. However, more of this later.

To turn to facts—we did get Farm Lane the new bridge, with the help of the Work Progress Administration. We persuaded the State of Michigan to cancel the bonds on the Union Building and the stadium, thus precluding the possibility that future appropriations for educational purposes would have to be used to pay off those debts. The W.P.A. approved a massive work project to complete the stadium, as well as a series of other projects that involved the use of thousands of employees for long periods. For each month of their employment, the college received, in addition to the labor costs paid by the U.S. government, an amount of seven dollars per man per month of labor, which we used to buy building materials for those projects.

This was the way we completed the Union Building and built the Farm Lane Bridge and the Class of 1937 Band Shell. During those depression years, Michigan State was one of the largest beneficiaries in the state of the W.P.A. programs.

Certainly one of the most successful ventures of that period was the initiation of the so-called 'self-liquidating' building programs. How did the general idea originate, how was it developed, and with whose help and how was it 'sold' to the governing board?

When I returned to M.S.C. as secretary, Mary Mayo Hall had been recently completed, the result of an innovative idea developed by the Detroit Trust Company. Aware of the great need for dormitories for women at the college, the company officers convinced the president and the State Board of Agriculture that it was a sound idea to borrow the required money to build Mary Mayo through a bond issue, pledging the income from the rental of the building to pay the interest and retire the debt over a reasonable period of years. The bonds were to be sold through Detroit Trust.

The building had been completed and was in use. It was and still is a beautiful building, but it was not paying its way. The Detroit Trust Company proved to be a burden by involving itself in all the details of the dormitory's operations, not because it wanted to be difficult but because it was interested in getting its money back. The interest rate being paid by the institution was about six percent per year, substantially higher than prevailing rates. One of my first concerns was to get Mary Mayo Hall refinanced and to get control of it out of the hands of the Detroit Trust Company and into the hands of the college. We were convinced that with efficient management it could become a sound investment, and that future investments in residence halls actually could pay the interest on the money borrowed and retire the Mary Mayo debt over a reasonable period of time.

From this beginning grew the whole network of dormitory and married student housing that made the M.S.U. housing program the largest of its kind in the world. There were later other self-liquidating buildings—Jenison Fieldhouse, the enlarged stadium, the Men's Intramural Building, the music buildings and several others. For one of the bond issues, totaling several million dollars in construction costs, we were able to borrow six million dollars at a one percent interest rate—certainly a much easier debt to retire than one with an interest rate of six or seven percent or more. You must remember, too, that at the time banks did not pay interest on savings accounts. All one had when one put his money in the bank was the promise that the deposit would be returned safely. Fortunately, that day in banking is long since gone.

The extent of Michigan State's building program raised hackles at other educational institutions. Many skeptics generated a good deal of criticism, directed at M.S.C. and its president, predicting bankruptcy and other dire consequences. To counteract these predictions of doom, we placed signs on the front of each of the self-liquidating buildings, pointing out that this building was not built with tax funds and explaining exactly how each building was to be paid for. For years this was a matter of interest to visitors to the campus, and helped a great deal to counteract unwarranted criticism.

The Michigan State experience played a substantial role in making possible the building of dormitories and residence halls on university campuses all over America with money borrowed from banks, insurance companies, and private investors. The idea was copied almost immediately at the University of Michigan and at what were then known as the Michigan Teachers' Colleges—Western Michigan, Eastern Michigan, Central Michigan, Northern Michigan, Michigan Technological Institute and others.

Looking back, what do you now consider to have been the most significant decisions, innovations, and events of your tenure as secretary?

It would be better, I believe, for others to make such appraisals. I should make the point, however, that whatever significant innovations were made and whatever advances were accomplished, none would have been possible had it not been for the continuous support of President Shaw and the members of the State Board of Agriculture. M.S.C., and later M.S.U., was blessed with competent, able board members who had great interest in Michigan State. They had confidence in it and a sincere desire to make it into a truly distinguished university of high quality, across the board.

It was clear from the beginning of my appointment as secretary that we needed much more land for development. We had, counting the campus and adjacent farms, about 700 acres of land, most of which was required by the Agricultural College. Since the legislature was completely lacking in enthusiasm about buying land, if we had had to go through the legislature each time we bought a lot or farm, it would have taken years to accumulate the amount that was needed.

The board and President Shaw agreed with my recommendation that we expand the campus and farm site as fast as we could. We decided to move south, making the east boundary of the campus south of the Red Cedar River at Hagadorn Road; the west boundary of the campus was to be Harrison Road, south from Michigan Avenue. We wanted to acquire everything between the east and the west boundaries as rapidly as possible. We also decided to buy only through private negotiation, without the use of condemnation procedures.

During the period that I was secretary, and later when I was president, the university acquired a total of some 700c acres without ever condemning a single acre or a single lot. Sometimes it took a long time and much negotiation; sometimes we had to wait for people to die; sometimes we made it possible for the owners of the property to live in the houses after purchase, the land to be turned over to the university only after the current occupants had lived out their lives. After the permanent university site was extended south to Jolly Road, we decided to go south far enough to include what is now Interstate U.S. 96, making the south boundary Sand Hill Road.

When I left the university April 1, 1969, we had only one substantial piece of land on the desired list that the university had not purchased. That was the Box Farm, something over 160 acres, near the intersection of Collins and Jolly Road. One of my final recommendations to the board of trustees was that they should buy that property at an early date. The asking price was high and the property was not acquired. Mr. and Mrs. Box have since died, and were I still involved in the affairs of the university, I should give high priority to the acquisition of that property. (Since this was dictated, the board of trustees have completed arrangements for the purchase of this land.)

Trustees like Forest Akers, William Armstrong, William Berkey, Clark Brody, Gilbert L. Daane, Ben Halstead, James J. Jakway, Sarah Van Hoosen Jones, Lavina Masselink, Fred Mueller, Matilda Wilson, and many others (all deceased) and many trustees and former trustees who are still living—among them Frank Merriman, Stephen Nisbet, Connor Smith, and Don Stevens—made what is now Michigan State University possibly by their complete and continuous support.

If I were to suggest what I consider to be most important for the future of the university, I should put priority on a system that would assure that the board of trustees be constituted of men and women with a real interest in education, and a thorough, sympathetic understanding of the role of a university like Michigan State. I would hope for their sincere concern in making it into an institution dedicated to improving the quality of life for all citizens, whether enrolled on our campus or elsewhere, in the country or in the world. Such boards are essential to the mission of the land grant universities in serving the public for whom they were founded.

Time has demonstrated that the political process which members of the board of trustees must go through—that is, nominated by the political parties and then elected as a part of a partisan ticket—is not necessarily conducive to the highest quality administration for universities. Governor William Milliken indicated to me, some years ago, his willingness to recommend to the legislature that they remove the Board of Trustees of Michigan State University, the Board of Governors of Wayne State and Board of Regents at the University of Michigan from partisan politics by means of a constitutional amendment that would make membership on those boards subject to appointment by the governor and approval of the state senate. In my view this would be a long step in the right direction. I am disappointed to see no signs of action on this proposal.

When did you first consider the presidency of M.S.C.?
What do you recall of the circumstances, and how they

*developed? For example, were you encouraged by members
of the state board, faculty members, alumni, etc.? Was the
future of the college discussed extensively, both before and
following your appointment?*

I can deal with this very briefly. President Shaw had been a member of the faculty at Michigan State College since about 1902, had served for over forty years as professor of agriculture and dean of agriculture and three times as acting president; and then for thirteen years of his tenure was full-time president of Michigan State. Neither he nor the board had discussed retirement, but it was assumed that when he reached seventy or thereabouts, he would be looking toward it.

I had no discussion with any members of the board of trustees until a few days before the board meeting when they announced their choice as his successor. There obviously had been a substantial amount of discussion among all six of the board members about my appointment but I was never consulted, nor did I know that such discussions were taking place. Two or three days before the meeting at which the action was taken, a committee of the board came to see me and indicated that they were going to discuss President Shaw's retirement with him. When he decided his retirement date, they wanted to know, would I accept the presidency if the board offered it to me?

There was only this single discussion with me, and it was not suggested that any action would be taken at the next meeting of the board, but possibly at some future meeting. President Shaw later told me that he had no part in the board's consideration of my appointment as president. I was never aware of any discussions, public or private, about President Shaw's retirement or the designation of his successor. The board of trustees, at the same meeting in which they approved the retirement of President Shaw—effective at the end of the college year on June 30, 1941—appointed me as the president of the college as of July 1, 1941.

I may have been too close to the scene to know the true feeling but I believe that the board's choice met widespread approval—from faculty, students and all those interested in Michigan State. My only discussion with anybody about the presidency of Michigan State was the conversation with the committee of three members of the board, previously referred to. I did indicate to them that I was interested, but I know nothing about other discussions in which they may have been involved.

When the board offered me the position, I accepted it. After the board meeting, the announcements of the retirement of Mr. Shaw and the appointment of a new president were made at the same time. When President Shaw left the campus on the first of July and moved to his new home on North Harrison Road, he refrained completely from that day forward from participating in any way in affairs of the university. He was always interested in what was occurring on the campus but he never "dabbled" in university affairs in any way.

It was his superb cooperation with me that caused me to decide quite early that if I lived to retire, I would give the same kind of support to my successor. When I did retire, to accept the position in Washington as administrator of U.S.A.I.D., I returned only once to the campus until I was invited to do so by my successor. The only exception was for a meeting, at their invitation, with the committee preparing recommendations for presidential candidates to be presented to the board of trustees.

PART II
THE DEVELOPMENT
OF THE UNIVERSITY

You became president of Michigan State College July 1, 1941, on the eve of America's entry into World War II. The interruption of normal university operations gave you time to think and plan for the future of the institution. Looking back, would you now agree that you took office at a propitious time?

That is an easy question. Would I now agree that I took office at a propitious time? I have found, having lived almost seventy-five years, that one is required to perform on the stage where he is at the time, faced with whatever problems there are at the time. All times, I suppose, are propitious.

Long before the presidency of the college appeared as a possibility, I had decided to make my career at Michigan State, so long as the board wanted me to do so. There were opportunities for me to do other things, but I wanted to put all my interest, all my energy, all my limited competence into the university in East Lansing in whatever capacity the institution thought I could make a contribution.

I had spent some years, of course, as the Secretary of the State Board of Agriculture and as Secretary of the College. I have noted earlier what President Shaw's first assignments to me were. We were in daily communication about these and many other things, and I also had well-established relationships with the deans and other administrative officials of the college, as well as with the Extension Service and the Agricultural Experiment Station.

During my ten years in Agricultural Extension I covered the state of Michigan backward and forward. I was familiar with Michigan geography from personal experience and knew a great many people throughout the state not only in agriculture but in other fields. I traveled to every corner of the state and spent most of my time talking to audiences not only interested in agriculture and in the college, but to business groups, social groups, luncheon clubs, church groups, and people in and out of state government. I learned early that one could deal much better with legislators by meeting them in their hometowns rather than in the halls of the state capitol.

I made it a point to become acquainted with them in their own districts, whenever they invited me. So when the State Board of Agriculture appointed me to succeed President Shaw, it meant simply that I would go on doing much what I had been doing for the previous seven years, except that it would be as president rather than as secretary of the board and of the college.

When I became president on the first of July 1941, Sarah, my wife, and I, with our first child, Mary Elisabeth, were living in our own home on Rosewood Avenue, in the area known as the Glencairn Estates. Michigan State, like most universities, maintained a home for the president on the campus. That had been true throughout its history except during the tenure of President Frank Kedzie, who preferred to lives in his own home in Lansing. Those homes that previously housed the presidents had been eliminated to make room for the new dormitories for women.

When I took office, the house that Dr. Shaw had lived in as dean of agriculture and as president was about to be removed to make room for additional women's dormitories. Therefore, we moved back into the house in which the secretaries of the college usually lived. When I became secretary, I was unmarried and had no desire to live on the campus, so the house had been turned to academic uses and later served as a home for Governor Frank Murphy. The board decided to convert it back into a home for the president, and Sarah and I actually were in the process of moving back to the campus on Pearl Harbor Day, December 7, 1941.

Material in the files suggests strongly that you already had in mind a number of major changes in policies and procedures: liberalizing the curricula and upgrading the quality of the faculty, for example. How fully developed were those ideas at that time?

This question requires a broad, general answer. I had already spent a lot of time thinking about how Michigan State College might become a better university, by every measure except that its official name was Michigan State College. With the passage of the Morrill Act in

1862 by the U. S. Congress and its signature by President Lincoln, the people of the United States were committed to establish in each state at least one institution of higher learning whose principal object should be training in agriculture and the mechanic arts.

This concept was, of course, not new to Michigan. The legislature had already established Michigan Agricultural College in 1855, which opened its doors in 1857, planned on much the same pattern and with similar objectives. Half of the first forty-eight states incorporated their land grant colleges as part of a comprehensive state university. The other half established their land grant colleges as separate A. & M. colleges, after the Michigan pattern.

In 1941, it was clear that the separate land grant colleges, who were educating agricultural scientists, engineers, home economists, doctors of veterinary medicine, public school teachers, graduates in business and commerce, and in other areas characteristic of modern life, must offer them the highest quality courses in all the arts and all the sciences—something much more than vocational training alone. Land grant institutions, more than ever before, had to be committed to the kind of education to fit their graduates for places in the postwar world. Graduates of Michigan State would have to compete not only with graduates of the comprehensive state universities, but with those from the great private universities, for position and influence in this new, complex society.

The answer to the question "What were you planning?" is simple. Our objective was to mobilize the faculty, the alumni, the friends of the college, the people of the state who supported it, the students and their parents, and to try together to make Michigan State a distinguished university.

Long before I became its president, Michigan State had introduced comprehensive programs in liberal arts and humanities, in the basic and applied sciences, in the social sciences, and in other fields needed to provide its graduates with the broadest and best kind of education. The College of Liberal Arts was already in existence under the directorship of Dean Emmons; the School of Applied Science was in operation under the direction of Dean Ralph Huston. There was an excellent Music Department, an adequate Art Department, and other educational areas were being developed.

A Memoir

It was clear to me from my observations of other institutions that to achieve our objective would require much more than simply broadening or liberalizing the curricula. The upgrading of the total faculty was the key. No university is better than its faculty. Nor could a university attract a superior faculty without an adequate library, or without the laboratories and facilities required for distinguished teaching and research.

The first priority, then, was improving the quality of the faculty. In the years that I had been secretary, when I visited other land grant colleges and state universities, I was always impressed by their pride in their past, the results of the work of their distinguished faculty members. On most of these campuses, buildings, libraries, and other monuments venerated those members of the faculty or administration who had made it possible for the university to grow from humble beginnings to a major institution. I felt that Michigan State had missed something by not encouraging its faculty, alumni, students and the public to recognize that Michigan State, too, had a past to be proud of.

I joined Michigan Agricultural College first as a student and was a faculty member when the college went through a painful legislative and a grand jury investigation. That was another chapter in a series of events in which some good people were more or less discredited as they left the university. Michigan State had on its campus very few evidences of the many distinguished faculty members who played key roles in the development of the college. Somehow or other, we had to make Michigan State a place that students, faculty and alumni and friends of the college could be proud of.

As to the second part of the question, how fully developed were those ideas at that time?, I do not remember. I know that I had a model in mind of what I believed Michigan State could and should be and I know that I spent a lifetime trying to achieve it. And at least the beginnings of the concept were there by the time I moved into the president's office in July, 1941.

You had a number of strongminded individuals as your associates when you became president, especially among the deans. Were they sympathetic to your progressive ideas or did they need to be persuaded and convinced?

I was fortunate to begin with an able staff of administrators. Dean Lloyd Emmons, Dean Ernest Anthony, Dean Ralph Huston, Dean Ward Giltner, Dean Henry Dirks, Dean Marie Dye, and many others were good people. I am not going to attempt to enumerate all of them. They were not all equally distinguished, but they all had cast their lots with Michigan State and all of them wanted to help to make M.S.C. the best possible educational institution of its kind. They were proud of the progress made in the years immediately preceding 1941, and of the college's vigorous growth. Added funds from the legislature made it possible to begin upgrading the faculty by offering salaries more nearly competitive with those at comparable colleges and universities. The administration and faculty were also sympathetic to progressive ideas; many helped to generate even more progressive ideas. I do not mean to say that we always agreed one hundred percent on every item, but we all started off by recognizing that an institution as large as Michigan State was in 1941 had to be a cohesive whole if it were going to move forward. We started out by involving all of the deans and all of the other administrative officials in planning the future of the institution. That included department heads, as they were called in those days, as well as everyone else who had a contribution to make.

The point is that from the first day of my presidency, my objective was to try to get the whole university pulling together. I was convinced that the president or chief executive of any sizable organization could not be effective unless he could get most of the people in it traveling down the same road, in the same direction, at the same time. If the work of any large organization is to be limited to what its head can do himself, it is not going to accomplish very much. To build a university—or to build any other important entity—one must be able to harness the efforts, the insights, the competencies and the energies of a great many people and, most importantly, of the *best* people. One of the problems in building a university is often the unwillingness on the part of many administrators to surround themselves with the ablest and most qualified associates. The human inclination is to prefer those who will not outshine the boss.

I knew that if we were to try to build Michigan State with that kind of attitude, we would not get very far. We had to find the best people available, across the board, and they had to come to M.S.U. because they wanted to come. Even the best would not be useful unless they came to stay, and unless they dedicated themselves to helping to make the university as good as we could make it. There may have been people in high places or low places who were less competent than they should have been. But I do not think that anywhere in the university there were many who had reservations about our overall objectives. I was convinced then, and I am now, that the overwhelming majority were ready and willing to get on with the job of making Michigan State the best possible university of its kind.

Would you discuss your working relationship with the deans and major department chairmen; what they were at the first and how they developed over the years?

We had an organization called the Administrative Group that met in the board room adjacent to the president's office every Tuesday morning at 9:00. It was expected that the deans and the principal administrative officials would always be there. At these meetings we discussed the problems of the university, its aims and aspirations, its day-to-day work. The Administrative Group was the number one communications medium within the institution. Every dean had an opportunity at each meeting to tell the others about what was happening in his college, or what was being planned.

Because we did not have much money and none to waste, we decided at the outset that the university would have only one subject-matter department per discipline. We had to work out a coordinating system so that the sciences that had been in the College of Applied Science played an appropriate role in the colleges that were concerned with the utilization of the sciences: agriculture, engineering, home economics, veterinary medicine, etc. We were not going to have a department of English in half a dozen places in the institution and we were not going to have one kind of mathematics in the College of Science and Arts and another kind in engineering or economics. This pattern differed from that of most universities at the time, but it worked well in East Lansing and helped the institution move as quickly as it did.

The principal administrators who were not involved in teaching, research, extension, or otherwise directly in academic operations constituted the Breakfast Group. This included the President, the Provost, the Vice President for Business and the Treasurer, the person in charge of public information, the Secretary of the Univesity, the Dean of University Services, the University Attorney and a few others. They met regularly every Monday morning at 7:00 A.M., first in the Union Building and later in Kellogg Center. That did not mean 7:00 A.M. for breakfast; it meant they had their coffee and eggs before the meeting started at 7:00 A.M. These weekly meetings were part of the internal communications pattern of university business and became an important factor in the operation of the institution. Some objections were raised to the early hour—but experience demonstrated that there were very few competing events at that time of day.

As the institution became larger, the academic operation of the university centered in the Office of the Vice President for Academic Affairs—later termed the Office of the Provost. During my tenure, this office was held by four outstanding men: Thomas Hamilton, who left to become President of the State University of New York; Paul Miller, who resigned to become President of the Univesity of West Virginia; Clifford Erickson, who sadly died in office; and Howard Neville, who accepted an appointment as President of Claremont College shortly after my departure. Each was my alter ego.

In other words, we tried from the beginning to provide for adequate internal communication, not only vertically but horizontally. Up-and-down communication lines within a university are relatively easy to establish; the flow goes from teaching staff to department chairmen to deans to provost or president. It is much more difficult to establish and maintain across-the-board communication so that all parts of the univesity always know what they need to know. There is nothing more discouraging to morale than for staff members to learn for the first time, from reading a newspaper or from meeting somebody far away, what is happening at his own institution. We tried to avoid that. Perhaps we did not succeed one hundred percent, but we made a real effort, and that was an important factor in building Michigan State from 1941 to 1969. I think that relationships among deans, department chairmen, and administrative, teaching, and operating staff were good.

Since I lived at the university, I was able to get out on the campus early every morning. On Monday mornings, we had the breakfast group meeting but on other days I walked around the campus myself every morning after breakfast and got to my office by not later than 7:30 A.M. or a quarter to eight. When large building projects were under way, I walked through the construction projects every day. I walked over the farms and through the laboratories and tried to know what was going on throughout the institution. I was as much interested in what was happening in the physical plant as in the academic departments or in the administration of the institution.

> *One of your first decisions and one of far-reaching importance was to upgrade the academic quality of the faculty. Would you discuss the situation in that respect as you found it and how you went about accomplishing your objective?*

When I first became secretary, the salary situation was serious. Salaries had been substantially reduced for all staff members during the depression years and had not been restored. The first effort had to be to bring salaries and wages back to the pre-depression level. Most other colleges and universities had been able to do that, but M.S.C. salaries remained substantially lower than those of other comparable intitutions. When one starts behind, it is difficult to catch up because other universities are moving ahead too. So it was not a matter of merely closing a gap; we had to close a gap that would constantly widen if it were not quickly closed.

In addition, M.S.C. had no established retirement policy. One of our serious problems was the painfulness of our retirement process. It was not automatic; some people retired at a fairly early age and others went on until they died of old age. Nor did the college have a pension system. Most colleges and universities had already joined the old Carnegie Endowment plan—the Teachers Insurance and Annuity Association—a participatory program which combined university contributions with the individual's regular salary deduction. The University of Michigan, for example, had been a part of the Carnegie plan from its beginning, while the teachers colleges were in the State Teacher Retirement Program. The legislature was not inclined to appropriate substantial new funds for a retirement system that had been neglected for too long by M.S.C.

To buy into an ongoing pension funding operation is costly. We had to start modestly with a university-financed program that eventually provided a maximum retirement payment of $300 a month—not much even then. We also had to set the effective date of this plan ahead a few years, and make financial provision to pay pensions for all the people previously retired who were going to be put on the pension rolls immediately. To develop an actuarially sound program, starting from scratch, was not easy. Nevertheless, we moved as fast as we could into the T.I.A.A. retirement plan. This had the great advantage of moving with the faculty member as he moved, from one institution to another, so that he was not faced late in life with the loss of his accumulated retirement rights.

We started off with the conviction that as a faculty member or administrator retired or left for any reason, we must always replace him with the best there was, a policy which called for higher salaries than we had been paying. If we could not pay a fully competitive salary almost immediately, other institutions that could offer more, either in salary or in perquisites, could hire good people away from us. We were growing rapidly and were always recruiting additional faculty as well as seeking replacements.

If we were really going to make substantial progress in improving the faculty, we would have to recruit the brightest young people as soon as they finished their doctorates in the better graduate schools. Out of any group of ten new people, we assumed, there might be two or three who would become truly distinguished, several would be adequate, some would become discouraged and leave, and some would soon find that they were not interested in becoming really competent university teachers or researchers.

The success of our recruiting was demonstrated by the fact that if you look over the staff of Michigan State University, you will find a substantial number of the senior faculty, including many who have the most distinguished reputations, who were recruited as they left graduate school, and who came as instructors or assistant professors to make their reputations at Michigan State.

One of our great satisfactions was to see a substantial number of those who left us take responsible posts as deans, administrators, or presidents in high quality universities. At one time there were twenty or more presidents or principal executive officers of strong universities who had served earlier on the campus in East Lansing.

It was always difficult to see good people leave, but a university is in the person-building business, trying to produce able and competent people. When faculty members had attractive offers to go elsewhere where opportunities seemed to be better, and after I was satisfied they really wanted to leave I always recognized that every person should have the opportunity to determine the course of his existence. Sometimes I told them I thought they were making a mistake, and in some instances they would return and say something like "Dr. John, you were right, I did make a mistake." Many times the position they had held was filled and we had no vacancy, but many times we did invite them back. I do not have to look very hard to find several distinguished members of the staff of Michigan State who left us for a time, decided to come back, and then had long and useful careers as part of the university family.

One of the real problems of higher-level administration of any complex institution, particularly at a university, is that of acquiring adequate management either by producing your own first-rate people or by recruiting experienced administrators. If you start with bright, well-trained, ambitious persons who will work hard, you have better material to start with. But one of the difficulties in a university is the fact that too often the promising young person finds the road to advancement closed because the upper-ranking professorships are filled.

At Michigan State we did pretty well, I think, in attacking this problem. We really tried to identify promising young people and we tried to provide them opportunities for growth; in this way many people with distinguished careers at M.S.U. or at other institutions were encouraged to realize their full potential by being given the chance to move up, perhaps in other areas of work in other departments and with other responsibilities. That is part of the job of building a university.

One of the decisions you made, for which you were not given enough credit, was to improve the economic status of the faculty by providing so-called fringe benefits in the way of pensions, stricter tenure policies, etc. Would you like to comment on that aspect of your early administration?

Some of this I mentioned earlier. I might emphasize again that in addition to providing competitive salaries, it is important to see to it that younger faculty are given full credit for everything they do well and are not unduly penalized every time they make a mistake. We tried always to recognize outstanding performances by commending the people personally, by writing them brief letters, or finding other ways to encourage them. We always tried, when someone made a substantial error, not to handicap him because of it. I usually would say, "Well, we didn't do that one very well, did we?" and say nothing more about it. For the right kind of person this was enough, and the mistake was not likely to be repeated. On the other hand, if too many mistakes came too often, it meant one had to take another look at that person's future role.

The non-academic sector of a university is important, too. We learned early that if we brought people in to manage dormitories or to be involved in the business end of the institution, it was to our advantage to seek those who had some knowledge about or interst in Michigan State—preferably former students or former employees who had demonstrated the required professional competencies, or management skills. I soon found that it was a mistake to put academics without business experience into positions requiring practical business ability unless they had already shown that they had the necessary qualifications. Former students who have succeeded in business can be invaluable; Emery Foster, Leslie Scott, and Arthur Brandstatter are examples of alumni who returned to Michigan State University in key roles and performed superbly. Their previous practical experience in dealing with the kinds of activities in which they were going to be engaged at M.S.U. was a great asset.

We made another decision early in the game—that if we had on-campus teaching programs in a field in which we were employing somebody from outside, we ought always to look first to our own teaching department for advice. For example, when I first came to the university we had a well established teaching program in landscape architecture which had no connection at all with the staff who were planning the campus. Years earlier the university had started the practice of hiring commercial outside planners to advise it with reference to location of buildings, landscaping arrangements, and the like.

T. G. Phillips was the outside consultant employed by the university—a graduate of M.S.C. who had done well in Detroit and elsewhere in the commercial landscaping business. His advice was excellent, but the first time there was an opportunity to bring someone from the Department of Landscape Architecture into the discussions to give direction to campus planning and landscaping, I did so. Later, after a lot of searching to find a landscape architect with a practical background, we turned to another M.S.U. graduate, Harold Lautner, who had unusually effective non-academic experience. He was made head of Landscape Architecture and Urban Planning and given the responsibility for campus planning. He did a superb job.

> *Much of this was accomplished or well started before the end of World War II and the dramatic upsurge in enrollment at the end of the war. Who were your principal supporters, defenders, willing workers, etc., in those early years? Who made up the opposition and how did you overcome opposition?*

First, I would have great difficulty in identifying the opposition. There probably were some who had less enthusiasm than others, but if any significant number of the faculty or friends of the university felt there was something seriously wrong with what the university was planning or doing, we took another look at it. We wanted to make certain that the critics were not right; if their criticism was valid, we moved to correct what was improvable as soon as possible.

It would be a mistake for me to list principal supporters or defenders or willing workers—practically everybody who was part of the institution would qualify. When progress is made in building something, everybody is more or less enthusiastic about it. There are not many critics. If there are you can overcome their criticisms best by demonstrating to them that what is being done is right. I found that you never get very far in trying to prove that a critic is wrong, if he is right.

I was often criticized—sometimes correctly—but if I were criticized in person or in the press or on the platform, I did not jump to defend myself until I took a look to see if the critic was right. I have often said that I learned very little from people who commended me, but I learned a heck of a lot from people who pointed out where we could do things better. One can learn much more from the honest critic than from the person who tells you what a great job you are doing when perhaps you are not.

My basic philosophy always has been not to be much interested in what *has* happened. The most important days are tomorrow and the days after that. If you waste time applauding yourself or listening to others applaud you, you use up time that ought to be spent getting ready to do better.

I learned early that it is difficult to make anything appear to be better than it really is. Many at M.S.U. got discouraged in the early years—and I suppose in later years too—when those on and off campus did not recognize what was being done well. Some may have thought that they did not get adequate publicity, or that we were much better than other people thought we were. I felt from the beginning that we would not get very far by using Madison Avenue advertising tactics in trying to sell the university.

If Michigan State was really a good institution, if it had excellent programs and distinguished faculty members and produced good graduates, I believed that sooner or later this would be recognized. The reputation of a university lags long after the fact. A university has to be a distinguished university for a long time before its peers—the responsible people at other institutions—will recognize that it *is* good.

There is the other side of the coin, of course. A university that has once been distinguished, and then simply rests on its reputation, will continue to be recognized as a good institution long after the procession has gone by.

What about the movement to liberalize the curriculum at Michigan State? There was much faculty sympathy for that movement, and some steps had already been taken toward it. Did someone sell that idea to you, or were you already in sympathy with it? What influence did Professor Floyd Reeves have on your thinking in this respect? Would you like to comment generally upon his services to you and to Michigan State?

First, I am happy to give Floyd Reeves full credit. If I were to identify a single individual to whom I think is due as much or more credit than any other single person for his contribution to making Michigan State move from what it was in 1941 to the kind of institution it was in 1969, I would put Floyd Reeves at the head of the list. When I first came to know him he was Dean of Education at the University of Chicago, with a distinguished academic record. He had played a key role in government during the Roosevelt administrations and had been called upon to do many important things. He was also a very practical fellow. He had been born and raised in a sod house in South Dakota, in an area where there was no primary school. Taught as a boy by his mother, he secured an education in the hardest way, and early in life achieved the distinguished reputation he fully deserved.

I first persuaded him to come to East Lansing as a consultant in 1943, first for one day a month, then one day a week, and eventually for a few months at a time. Finally I succeeded in persuading him to leave his tenured position at the University of Chicago and come to Michigan State full time. I told him that I thought he could have a more profound effect for good on the lives of more people, and bring about more improvements in the world as a full-time member of the staff at Michigan State than he could at the University of Chicago or anywhere else.

Floyd Reeves' greatest strength was his ability to take a group of people who did not agree on much of anything, start asking questions and keep asking them, and listen to their answers. He kept the questions and answers going, so that over a period of a few hours, days, or weeks they would change their thinking and become full participants in dealing with the problems at hand.

During the early days of my presidency the war was on and our faculty had few regular students. We had women students, some men who could not qualify for military service, and large numbers of military students from the Army and Air Force. All of our facilities were fully used, and our dormitories, fraternities, and sororities were taken over for military personnel. Many members of our faculty were teaching courses designed for the military, rather than university courses of the prewar type.

This was a good time, I believed, to begin to look at Michigan State and to plan for the kind of university that we hoped it was going to be after the war. We knew there would be substantial increases in enrollment. By 1945 there had been five or six consecutive classes of high school graduates who had all gone into the military service; when the war was over, many of them were going to flock back to universities or colleges. No one knew, then, that the federal government would institute the G.I. Bill and provide subsidized education for all returning veterans who wanted it.

So we started looking at what we had been doing. Here we involved Floyd Reeves and some of our best faculty who were interested in making Michigan State better than it had been. We used a technique that we later used very widely, that of appointing a committee of bright people from all of the colleges across the whole university. Some were academic conservatives and some were progressives, but their first objective was to figure out what it was we were trying to do educationally. It is relatively simple to accomplish an objective if you understand what the objective is, but very difficult to accomplish much that is constructive if you are uncertain what it is you are aiming at. The aim of the first study, out of which the Basic College came, was to establish what kind of education the average Michigan State student—from Detroit or some other Michigan city, or from a Michigan farm or small town—would need. We were not uninterested in out-of-state or out-of-country students, but we thought our primary emphasis should be on those from Michigan.

What kind of an education was he or she going to need to fit him or her for a useful and satisfying role in the life of the postwar years? Obviously, all of our graduates would need to know much more than before about the kind of world they would be living in, but that was a secondary consideration. Our first was to give the student the best education we could for a full, useful life.

Out of this effort, out of all the discussions and committee meetings, came the notion that we needed a program that was all inclusive, one in which all freshmen and sophomores would be exposed to the kinds of knowledge that every educated person *should* be exposed to. Then, if they went on to be agricultural scientists or engineers or teachers or home economists or medical students or business persons or whatever, they could then specialize. First, though, we believed they all should be *generally* educated.

There had been, of course, previous efforts to liberalize the electives offered in agriculture and engineering and other curricula. They did not work very well, because the professionals in the various fields tended to put the highest priority on specialization. For example, the tendency had been to keep the young engineer who did not do well in mathematics in engineering, until he had accumulated such a poor record in mathematics that it was difficult for him to transfer to another field. Experience showed that prospective engineers who had difficulty in mathematics might do well in other fields. The same thing could be said about the students who did not do well in chemistry and who, therefore, had trouble in pre-medicine, agriculture, or elsewhere.

After months of diligent effort the faculty committees under Reeves' leadership, came up with recommendations for a required two-year program common to all freshmen and sophomores. Originally, there were seven basic courses, of which all students were required to take five.

It was remarkable that our diverse faculty voted without a single no vote to create a new Basic College (later known as University College) for every freshman and sophomore, under the supervision of a separate faculty. Each student had the opportunity, while completing Basic College requirements, to enroll in the prerequisite courses required for those seeking degrees in the upper colleges. Harvard and a few other universities had general education programs but they were optional; if a student was bright enough and experienced enough to elect the kind of general education that we *required* through our Basic College, the probabilities were good that he did not need it.

To return to Floyd Reeves. He played a major role in creating the Basic College but he had good material to work with. If the faculty and the administrators of Michigan State had not been forward-looking and open-minded and dedicated to building a university designed to achieve its own objectives without reference to what was being done at Ann Arbor or Ohio State or Harvard or California-Berkeley or somewhere else, we would not have been able to do what we did.

Our people became convinced that what other universities were doing might be interesting, but not necessarily right for Michigan State. But the old M.A.C. attitude was well exemplified by the distinguished professor of botany, Dean Ernst Bessey, who repeatedly at faculty meetings would ask the question, "Is there precedent for this?" And if Chicago or Michigan or Harvard or Stanford was doing something that we suggested, why, of course, that was all right. But if there was not an example somewhere else, if a so-called major university was not doing exactly what we proposed, then in the view of Dr. Bessey and others, it should be forgotten.

M.S.C. had overcome that attitude by the postwar years. Under the leadership of Reeves and others, our faculty was convinced that if they tried to out-Harvard Harvard, they were not going to succeed. And if they were not careful, they might find in the process that the objectives Michigan State had been designed for would not be achieved. Our university had reached the point where it could move in the direction it should to become truly distinguished.

In giving Floyd Reeves full credit for his contribution, I should point out others who deserve recognition. One was Howard Rather, who had been professor of Farm Crops in the College of Agriculture when he became the first Dean of the Basic College. He gave it excellent leadership, but unfortunately he died at a much too early age. Ernest Melby came to M.S.U.'s College of Education with a brilliant record and gave the university years of magnificent service, particularly by his contributions to the College of Education. Some others from outside were only with us for a little while, like Dean Potter, the long-time Dean of Engineering at Purdue, who spent a year or more here when we were reviewing our engineering program and looking for a new dean. His services were invaluable. The trouble is once you start to pick out a few for credit you pass over a great many others of equal or greater merit. So let us leave all this to another day.

You recognized from the beginning the need for improving the library resources. Do you recall how we stood in that area in comparison with the institutions with which we were or would be competing as Michigan State acquired status as a major univeristy? What plan of action was adopted and pursued?

The library at Michigan State in the early days of my presidency was pretty puny. After we became a member of the Big Ten, the situation was even more embarrassing because in library facilities we were a poor tenth among ten. We had to do something about that.

First of all, we decided that we could not get along without a much better library. The library is the heart, nerve center and intestinal tract of a university. As we began to move into graduate education, it was absolutely essential that we have a top-level library, with better facilities, more space, much more money, and a different kind of management. Without criticizing any individual, it has seemed to me that some librarians have the instincts of a chipmunk. Their idea is to gather together a lot of books and then store them away where they will be carefully preserved and protected from use.

We knew that our library must have available all titles and publications needed for students and faculty and off-campus users. It is absolutely useless to measure the value of a library by the number of volumes or the number of titles on the shelves—what counts is the use that is made of what is there. We knew from the beginning that it was going to cost a great deal of money. A library does not have much sex appeal; it is difficult to get a legislature to provide adequate funding for something that costs as much as the kind of library Michigan State needed. But we did make progress, though the library no doubt still needs more resources than it has.

Reorganizing the structure of the university—establishing colleges and shifting departments—was going on continually in the early years. Your comments on this area, planning and prosecution.

To answer this adequately would require taking the university apart, college by college, dealing first with the College of Agriculture, then the Colleges of Engineering, Home Economics and Veterinary Medicine, Science and Arts, the College of Business, the College of Medicine and the Communication Arts, etc. Since to write that history would require much reading and much documentation, I shall not go into detail.

As I have indicated, the university was always in motion. It started as a small college emphasizing agriculture and mechanical arts. In 1941, and after, it aspired to be much better than it ever had been. It grew into a distinguished university, with a large faculty, some 40,000 students, reasonably adequate facilities, and financing, and a student body that had been greatly upgraded—an institution generally recognized, not only in Michigan but in the United States and the world as a highly respectable university. There was no blueprint in the beginning, nor was there a frozen blueprint when I left in 1969. Our attitude has been that we should always be studying ourselves, revising our aims, reassessing our responsibilities.

It makes no difference what college one might be talking about. The College of Agriculture should be concerned with doing the best possible job of training undergraduates and graduates in agriculture, in carrying on the research essential to Michigan's and the nation's and the world's needs. The Extension Service must serve not only the farmers of the state and the people who live in rural communities but city dwellers too. All colleges at M.S.U. have always been encouraged to continually reexamine their programs with an eye toward improvement.

As I assumed the presidency of what was then M.S.C., I believed that our first priority was to figure out what it was that the institution wanted to be at the end of the war and beyond. The faculty, the administration, the State Board of Agriculture (now the Board of Trustees) and the people of the state through the legislature, all were involved in planning the development of a college into a university.

It soon became clear that the people of Michigan expected Michigan State to have a broad perspective, something wider than the East Lansing campus. Anything that we could provide—credit or non-credit, off-campus or on-campus—that had educational value, anything that helped people to earn a better living or live a better life, we considered legitimate. Michigan State, we hoped, should broaden people's horizons so that they might better understand the world they were part of, and might discover how to make their own lives meaningful and worthwhile. This kind of thinking, for example, caused us to move into the continuing education program with the help of the Kellogg Foundation and the foresight of Emory W. Morris and the others who encouraged us in the early days.

To philosophize a bit, it is my contention that governments exist to provide the kinds of services and opportunities that make it possible for the largest possible number of people to develop the potential that God gave them so that they may make the maximum useful contribution to the society of which they are a part. This is the thinking that justified public education in the first place, that created public primary schools, secondary schools, colleges and universities. Political, social and economic systems change, but the basic role of education does not.

The purpose of education is to take all young people at the earliest possible time in their lives and make available to them the full range of opportunities—in school or out of school—that will help them grow into useful persons. When the young person completes the education available in the local community—at one time in the past the grade school, then the high school, and often the community college—it becomes the responsibility of the university to take over. Anything that comes within the definition of education—defined broadly—should be worthy of thoughtful consideration by a university. With the widening of horizons to which Michigan State committed itself, it was absolutely essential that there be constant change and constant growth.

We always encouraged this kind of sustained search for improvement. If we were bright enough to think of something that we should be doing, or to figure out a better way of doing what we hoped to do, we tried to get on with it. There was no reason why we could not take something apart and put it together again if by so doing we could do better than before.

> *What about physical development. Your critics concede that you were a builder in the sense of development of physical facilities, much as they ignore your contributions in the academic field. But without buildings, the one-time college could never have developed into a major university. Explain the planning for new buildings and other facilities during the war years, with the result that we were far more advanced than any other Michigan institution in preparation for returning veterans.*

It is certainly true that without the additional buildings what was Michigan State College could not have become Michigan State University. But before discussing the planning for new buildings and other facilities, it would be well to take a few minutes to recall the background.

Shortly after I became Secretary of the College and Secretary of the Board of Agriculture, the board approved a recommendation by President Shaw making me responsible for the buildings and grounds, their maintenance, their repair, alterations, construction of new buildings, etc., an assignment I considered to be very important.

I thought that the best thing to do first was to find out how buildings had been planned in the past, including the minor structural changes provided for in the annual budgets under alterations and improvements. I learned what I could about the procedures used in the planning of buildings at other large universities and public institutions, how contracts were let, how construction was supervised, and so on.

The college had a continuing arrangement with a Lansing firm of architects headed by Edward Bowd, who had been in the architectural business for a long time. He had working with him a younger architect named Orley J. Munson. Since Munson was frequently on campus, I used every opportunity to become familiar with the best way to use the skill and know-how of professional architects. I studied the structures on campus, those designed by Bowd-Munson and those designed by other architects. Since the university's relationship with Mr. Bowd was of long standing, most of the buildings had either been planned by, added to, or altered by his firm.

Beaumont Tower, however, had been designed by the Albert Kahn Company of Detroit. The Kahn Company were internationally known architects and had been selected by John Beaumont, who provided the funds for the construction of Beaumont Tower as a memorial to the M.S.C. men who lost their lives in World War I and earlier wars. Mr. Beaumont had been a long-time member of the Board of Agriculture and was an alumnus of M.A.C. Kedzie Chemistry Building was designed by an architectural firm in Detroit, known as Malcolmson and Higginbotham; the person with whom we dealt in that firm was Ralph Calder. Later the firm became Malcolmson, Higginbotham and Calder, and eventually as the older architects retired, the Ralph Calder Associates.

In those days the campus was not very large and I made it a practice every morning to walk over much of the campus to see what was going on. If construction was taking place, either of new buildings or substantial alterations, I made it a point to check its progress practically every day. The Buildings and Grounds Department reported to me as secretary and after I became president I kept up my interest in its work, until I was certain that my successor as secretary, Karl H. McDonel, would continue to give the physical plant and the grounds his best attention.

I acquired from Tommy Gunson part of my early interest in campus planning. When I came to M.A.C. as a student, Tom Gunson lived in a house adjacent to the Botanic Gardens and took care of the Botanic Gardens and the Herbarium. He had a great interest in plants, and in the planning and maintenance of the campus grounds. Also, my grandfather, Alfred Hannah, was a florist, flower grower and market gardener in Grand Rapids. My father was associated with him in the early years and then had his own greenhouses and market garden. He was interested in botany and horticulture and I learned a great deal from him. Therefore, I naturally grew up with a life-long interst in trees, shrubs, plants, birds and wildlife. I had been interested from the days of my first acquaintance with the campus in preserving it as an unusual teaching laboratory for students and the public. But let us return to the planning of new buildings and other facilities during the war years.

After 1941 the college became, in effect, a military camp. We had women students and a large number of men in uniform, some Air Force and some Army students in other military training programs. At the same time, as I mentioned earlier, we were planning the new Basic College, to be ready for the students who would arrive after the war. We knew it would not be successful, nor would our other programs, if we did not have classrooms, laboratories and libraries of the kind it required. In the early planning stage, we were not thinking about specific types of buildings or building locations. We began by trying to predict what kinds of facilities we would need for whatever number of students there were to be.

We were blessed during these difficult years with a very effective State Board of Agriculture consisting of six members, dedicated people, devoted to planning for a better university. They were, as at present, nominated by the political parties and elected by statewide vote. It had been the policy of both parties to select outstanding persons as candidates for the State Board of Agriculture. Board members participated actively in discussions about the M.S.U. of the future, and were committed to making the university ready, when the war was over, to take care of our share of students. We knew that the state government, the federal government and the majority of Michigan citizens were equally committed to the idea that there would be a very important role in postwar society for colleges and universities like Michigan State. We assumed that there would be not only students like those enrolled before the war, most of them from the state of Michigan, but we assumed too that many of the men who had been at M.S.U. in uniform, even though they might be from California, New York, Florida or elsewhere, might return to the East Lansing campus.

Our thinking about the buildings that might be needed in this program or that program was quite preliminary at that point. We continually discussed our plans with Mr. Munson and Mr. Calder, who were retained as consulting architects, and went ahead to plan for sewers and water and electrical power and heat with Consumer's Associates of Jackson, our consultants in these matters. So we knew what we were going to do, and were ready to move when the war ended.

Would you recall your experiences with Governor Kelly in the Victory Building Program, and with Senator Bishop and Representative Espie?

The State of Michigan was fortunate in having Harry F. Kelly as governor during this period. He was a vigorous, active person, a veteran of World War I, and a practicing attorney in Detroit. While he was a product of the Catholic parochial schools and the University of Notre Dame, he was a great supporter of public education. He, too, had made up his mind that when the war was over, he would see to it that Michigan took care of its returning veterans as effectively as possible. As governor, Harry Kelly was a vigorous spokesman for high quality education from kindergarten through graduate school, and as he became more acquainted with Michigan State, he became more interested in it.

I knew him as a personal friend. He was helpful on many occasions, not only in advancing the cause of Michigan State, but in other ways. When Governor Kelly decided that there was going to be a state victory building program and that there would be funds for it made available to universities who knew what they wanted, we bestirred ourselves and got out of the pigeon holes all the plans that we had been thinking about for so long. We made our wants known, and because our plans were precise, well thought out and sensible, the governor and the legislature treated us fairly. I do not mean that we had preferential treatment. Since we had already thought about it earlier, we were able to put together quickly the plans and the specifications and the illustrative materials that would be persuasive in convincing the governor, the legislature and the taxpayers.

John Espie and Otto Bishop were key Michigan legislators. Mr. Bishop was the Chairman of the Senate Appropriations Committee and Mr. Espie was the Chairman of the House Appropriations Committee. They were helpful and supportive, quite typical of the attitude of most of the members of the legislature at that time. The people of Michigan wanted to provide adequate educational opportunities not only for veterans, but for all of Michigan's sons and daughters, and the legislators reflected this.

Please explain how the self-liquidating building program was related to other building projects, and how much it meant to the growth of the university.

Since I discussed the self-liquidating program earlier I will only recall that we built residence halls and other kinds of structures with borrowed money to be repaid, interest and principal, out of earnings or dedicated income. The fact that we had this experience made it easier for us to plan for dormitories and married student housing. We knew we could finance those projects with borrowed money, so we did not have to go to the legislature for approval, except to report what we were pledging and how and why.

The self-liquidating program, of course, meant a great deal to M.S.U. Without it we could not have built our student housing. Without the residence halls and married housing, we could never have accommodated the returning veterans and their families. And without the classrooms and the laboratories and the libraries, we would not have had the educational facilities that were required. They were all tied together.

One of the experiments which paid off especially well was our decision in the early sixties to combine student housing, faculty offices, and library and laboratory facilities in the same building. In the first place, since these were self-liquidating projects, we would gain faculty and instructional space that we would not have been able to finance in separate buildings. Second, it was obviously more efficient to move a smaller number of faculty to the students than to move larger numbers of students to the faculty. In addition, we believed that we could give our students a valuable small-college experience within the context of a large university; a substantial number of first- and second-year students would live together, take classes together in the same building and, in effect, feel a kind of group solidarity. Case Hall, the first of these resident-instruction dormitories, was completed in 1962; Wilson, the next, also in 1962; and Wonders in 1963. They are still in existence and have been widely copied elsewhere.

Your close associates thought at times that you were almost obsessed in your insistence on purchasing more and more open land. Will you explain the rationale for your program of land acquisition for the university?

From the time I first became associated with M.A.C. I believed that if it was going to grow up to its potential, it was going to need much more land. In order to provide the kind of community atmosphere that would be conducive to the development of a first-class university, we would have to clean up some of the areas close to the campus that it did not then own or control. Land grant colleges, with their operating farms, were usually located in farm communities. When cities grew up around them, the farm acreage was needed for campus buildings, so that there eventually was little or no land left for the use of the college of agriculture. As a result, colleges of agriculture were sometimes forced to go out many miles, to acquire new land. This was not a good arrangement. One either moved the agricultural college or the students away from the campus. Shifting the agricultural activities away from the university made difficulties for the college of agriculture and deprived the university of one of its great strengths. It would certainly be advantageous if the agricultural college could have its farm land adjacent to the university for both its research and demonstration facilities.

We knew, too, that since we were going to need housing for large numbers of students, the residence halls should be located over an area wide enough to avoid student congestion in any one place on the campus. If the campus was to continue to serve as an important educational asset, then the old Campus Park north of the river should be preserved. That this great living classroom had been built and maintained was due largely to the work of men like Professor Beal, Tommy Gunson, Dr. Bessey, T. G. Phillips and many others interested in exhibiting on campus all the varieties of trees, shrubs, and woody plants that could be made to grow in Michigan. All of our planning indicated that the total campus area would have to be greatly enlarged.

I learned early that it was very difficult for the college to acquire land. By previous practice, the legislature had to be consulted every time the college intended to purchase a lot or a farm, which meant long delays and public discussions of purchase arrangements and prices. It could become very complicated as land owners, involved in feathering their own nests, tried to get asking prices increased. Therefore, before the war, President Shaw asked me to see if we could not work out different arrangements with the legislature. That was not easily done, but it finally agreed that since the State Board of Agriculture was an independent constitutional corporation, there was no reason it needed to discuss with the legislature whether or not the college should acquire ten acres or one hundred acres more land, any more than the board needed legislative approval for courses to be taught or textbooks to be used. And so it was arranged that we should report to the legislature from time to time what the board was proposing to do in the way of land acquisitions and then be ready to answer questions, if they were asked.

Our enlightened board was a great help. First, we needed to buy up nineteen old houses on the site now occupied by Kellogg Center and add that area to the university property across the river. Something also needed to be done about the old community public dump on the west side of Harrison Road where the Brody dormitories are now located. It was an unsightly thing, with great piles of rat infested trash and scavengers constantly digging into the rubbish. Immediately south of the Kalamazoo Street entrance and north of the Grand Trunk tracks there were several tracts of land that were not owned by the university, one or two of some size. M.S.U. owned no land on Harrison Road south of the railroad tracks. We wanted to purchase all the land we could between Harrison Road on the west and Hagadorn Road on the east and south, first to Mt. Hope Road and later south to Jolly Road—hundreds of acres in that area. We began these purchases when enrollment began to grow at a rapid rate immediately after the war, jumping from a prewar enrollment of 6,000 students to more than 15,000 within two or three years afterwards. The board agreed that much of the property north of Mt. Hope Road, previously devoted to farms and agriculture, would be required for added teaching facilities and that dictated the amount of land the university should acquire for farm and agricultural purposes.

About that time the State Highway Department was in the early stages of planning an interstate highway immediately south of the campus. It was first proposed that what is now I-96 would cross the campus north of Mt. Hope Road. It was helpful to the M.S.U. cause that the Secretary of Commerce in President Eisenhower's cabinet at that time was Fritz Mueller, a former member of our Board of Trustees. The Bureau of Public Roads were responsible to him and when it appeared that I-96 might cross the campus and block its development, we were able to exercise some influence through him. In the final decision, I-96 was located much farther south than had been originally anticipated. M.S.U. could then extend its holdings to Sand Hill Road, so that the university would control the land on both sides of I-96 south to Sand Hill Road.

Particularly important was the decision made by the trustees, when we were discussing land purchases with the legislature, that the university would not use the right of eminent domain, that is, the right to condemn property for university purposes. Condemning land for public purposes is a common practice with state institutions, but it does little to increase the popularity of the institution with its neighbors. The university's decision that it would acquire land only through private purchase meant that every acquisition was privately negotiated. Private negotiations may take a long time, are often discouraging, and sometimes irritating. But in the end, buying land this way was well worth it. M.S.U. was able to say that no person had his land taken from him without his approval, and that he always received a price that satisfied him.

Perhaps it would be useful for me to remind readers that when I first knew the college the dairy barn was on the north side of the river and so were the veterinary college facilities, the college orchards, most of the college vegetable gardens, the vineyard, the asparagus patch, and much else. The poultry houses, too, were on the north side of the river where the Physics Building, Psychology Building and other buildings now stand. Where the Shaw Dormitory, the College of Business, Chemistry and the rest of that complex is now located was cow pasture for the dairy herd.

A good deal of time, effort and energy was expended over the years in making certain that the university had a site adequate for its future needs. We took the long view, not only for a few years, but for one or two hundred years and beyond. A good many people thought we were overly ambitious, that we were trying to look down the road too far. I never backed off. I never lost my conviction and I am certain that we were right.

Another program close to your heart was the planning of the campus and the enhancement of its aesthetic beauty. Would you comment on that program from which the university today benefits so much?

I believed in the beginning, I believed all the time I was president and I believe today that one of the university's greatest assets is the beautiful park in which the campus is located. This is not accidental. It exists due to the foresight and good judgment of many people long since gone.

Long ago it was planned that the campus should be an outdoor laboratory, with all the varieties of trees and shrubs and woody plants that could be made to grow in Michigan, labeled and tagged not only for the students in botany and silviculture and landscape architecture, but for all students and faculty and people in the community. Life can be much more interesting and satisfying for those who understand that human beings are biological organisms in a biological world and who can tell one tree from another, one shrub from another, one plant from another, distinguish birds and their songs and know something about the wild animals that God placed here. I commend the trustees and the present management of the university for its work in maintaining the parklike atmosphere of the M.S.U. campus, for making it no less beautiful than it always has been and no less a part of the total educational operation.

If the management of M.S.U. in the years ahead will maintain the park that is the present campus, it will perform a great public service for those who will be here long after we are gone. If people born and raised in apartment houses in the cities find themselves on a univeristy campus where they can walk leisurely among trees, shrubs, birds, and flowers, they may be inspired to learn something about the facts and forces of nature that add significance to human life.

His first appointment, John Hannah as an extension agent. *Ca* 1923.

Board Meeting, *L-R* Melville B. McPherson, Forest H. Akers, James J. Jakway, Mrs. Lavina Masselink, President Robert S. Shaw, William H. Berkey, Clark L. Brody, Secretary John A. Hannah, Charles O. Wilkin. *Ca* 1940.

G. I. Bill veterans housed in Jenison Field House. 1946.

The Quonsets. 1947.

The building of Kellogg Center for Continuing Education. 1951.

Serving as Assistant Secretary of Defense, Hannah eats Thanksgiving dinner with infantry troops during a 1953 visit to South Korea.

Spring Commencement 1951.
L-R Nelson A. Rockefeller, John A. Hannah, Alexander E. Ruthven.

Addressing the first graduation class of the University of Nigeria.
Vice-Chancellor George Johnson is on Hannah's left. October, 1960.

Akhter Hamead Kahn with Hannah during a planning visit to Pakistan. 1961.

His twenty-fifth anniversary dinner.
L-R Mrs. Hannah, John Hannah, Durwood P. Varner. 1966.

In his office in the old Administration Building.

Speaking at Spring Commencement. June, 1979.

PART III
UNIVERSITY
ADMINISTRATION

*The role of the trustees is not always fully understood, even
by trustees. Would you describe that role ideally?*

First, I will speak in general terms about trustees and their role
in the management of a university. Under the Michigan Constitution the trustees are co-equal with the legislature, not subservient to
it. They are given sole and exclusive responsibility for the government of the university. They are charged with the selection of the
president of the university, who is the executive officer of the university in all of its parts. This system of university management does
not work well if the trustees involve themselves directly in internal
administration.

The role of the board of trustees of the university should be likened
to that of a board of managers or board of directors of a corporation.
The board hires the president. The trustees make the decisions to be
followed in the administration of the university. They approve the
budget. They act on all important appointments of personnel on the
recommendation of the president. They are free to call the attention
of the president to any management shortcomings or oversights. If
these are not corrected to the satisfaction of the trustees, theirs is the
final judgment.

This brings me to a discussion of the tenure of the president. There
is a growing inclination on the part of universities to hire presidents
for a fixed period of years. I was the president of Michigan State
University for the better part of twenty-eight years, without tenure;
I had given tenure to all university professors but had no fixed tenure
as president. It was always understood that the trustees at any board
meeting could employ a new president if they wanted to, reassign his
predecessor to a professorship, or retire him.

I think for the sake of the university that Michigan State's is the
better system. It is tough on the president, but he knows that when
he accepts the presidency. If he is given tenure as a professor, he has
all the security that he really needs. The ideal position in the whole
university hierarchy is that of the full-time senior professor. The full
professor has all the protection and all the privileges of his rank and

67

he has no more responsibility beyond the classroom or the research laboratory than he wants to carry.

To say the same thing in a different way, if I were to suggest how a university should be managed, I would start with a board of trustees all of whose members are interested in education, and who understand and support the role and purpose of a state university. Trustees set the tone for a university. They give the president the support he needs to carry out their policies and their decisions, whether philosophical, academic, or whatever.

It is not necessary for every board member always to agree with the president. The role of the board is to reach decisions by a majority vote. Once the majority vote has been determined, that becomes the policy of the university until it is changed, and it is changed only by another decision reached by a majority vote of the board. There need be no acrimony or bitterness over differences. Civilized people should be able to express their views in such a manner that even though sharp differences are held and vigorously expressed, disagreements can be left in the boardroom after the vote is taken. The most important role of the president is to promote, attain and maintain continuous communication with the members of his board. It is not fair to the board to be faced with the necessity of making decisions without first having had adequate opportunity to review all of the facts and all of the background material needed to arrive at intelligent conclusions.

When it comes to the routine administration of the university the president should be the principal executive officer at all times, except when the board is actually in session. His relationship with the faculty and staff, the legislature, the public and all others on behalf of the university should be conducted in a calm, dignified manner and with firmness and objectivity. He need not take strong public positions in speaking for the university on controversial issues unless he is assured of the consensus of his board. With a board of eight members, having five members on your side and three on the other is hardly a consensus.

It is much better if important decisions are not made until there is a consensus. That does not mean that all decisions need to be unanimous. There can well be one or two members of a contrary view, or in extreme cases, three members of a board of eight who have no real enthusiasm for the final conclusion. But once a determination has been made, it is expected that the full board will go along with it until a later majority is satisfied that it is wrong. Then a fresh vote can be taken if that seems desirable.

Finally, it is not my view that the trustees should ever be rubber stamps for the president. They should participate fully in all judgments on important policy matters, with the understanding that once a decision is made they will support it until a majority of the board members change their mind.

How close have our trustees come to filling that role?

In the early years of my presidency, almost all members came to the board of trustees understanding its responsibility and its role in the administration of the university. They were constant and dependable supporters of the university; they served well as a sounding board for ideas that came to them from the president or from other sources.

In the last few years of my tenure there were times when the situation was less pleasant. Now, after more than eight years have passed since I left the president's office, I think it should be generally recognized that all of my interests in Michigan State are as sincere now as ever, and as wholeheartedly supportive as they ever could be. I feel more free now to record my views frankly than I would have felt able to do earlier.

For the most part, all members of the board of trustees understood their appropriate role and complied with it. In the last few years of my tenure there were a few who had other ideas. This made life less agreeable for the administration than it had been before. But even during that period—right up to the last meeting of the board over which I presided in late March, 1969—there was never any question but that the majority of the members of the board always supported the president when he was right.

If the president asked for decisions or advice he was never offended if the board or individual board members disagreed with him, as they occasionally did. I participated in every regular meeting of the State Board of Agriculture and of its successor, the Board of Trustees, as its secretary or president from January 1, 1935 through March 31, 1969, a period of thirty-four years plus three months. The support of all of those boards made possible the development of M.S.U. from what it was to what it is today.

From your close relations with our board members for a period of thirty-four years, would you tell us about some of the individuals who served the university well, and what they did, how they performed?

During my tenure twenty-nine different elected members of the board served as trustees. Since superintendents of public instruction were also ex-officio members of the board of trustees through 1964, there were five incumbents of that office who served for a total of thirty-one years out of my thirty-five years as a member of the board. It is impossible to make comparisons among different board members. They had different qualifications and different interests. Each, in his own way, made substantial contributions to the university.

To do justice to the trustees, I should have to devote a separate chapter to each one. Instead, I can give only thumbnail sketches of those who stand out most clearly in my memory.

CLARK BRODY, of Lansing, was a member of the board for twenty-six of my thirty-five years; he had already served on the board for twelve years before I arrived as its secretary in January 1935. During much of that time he was chairman. He had a profound effect, all of it good, on the development of the university. For most of his career he was the manager of the Michigan State Farm Bureau and was a potent voice for Michigan agriculture and an active alumnus. He lived in Lansing and was always available for advice and counsel.

FOREST AKERS, of Detroit, was a member of the board for eighteen years. He was Vice President of the Chrysler Corporation and Sales Manager of Dodge Motors. Earlier he had been in charge of sales for Reo Motor Company of Lansing and before that for the Oliver Farm Machinery Corporation. No member of the board during my tenure was more generous with his time, energy and money in the service of M.S.U. He, too, was a dedicated alumnus who had been active as a student in athletics and retained his interest and enthusiasm. He left all of his estate in trust, with the income to be used to benefit the university.

CONNOR SMITH, a veterinarian from Arenac County and another alumnus of M.S.U., was a member of the board for sixteen years of my tenure. An active, constructive and always valuable trustee, he served for several years as chairman of the board.

WILLIAM BERKEY, of Cassopolis, editor and owner of the Cassopolis *Vigilant,* was a member of the board when I joined it and for another fourteen years, afterwards. He, too, was an effective chairman of the board for several years. As former President of the Michigan Press Associates, he was always active in the service of M.S.U. among the daily and weekly newspaper publishers of the State.

FREDERICK H. MUELLER, of Grand Rapids, also an alumnus, was a prominent civic leader in Grand Rapids, and later Secretary of Commerce in President Eisenhower's cabinet. He was a strong member of the board for thirteen years until he resigned to accept the cabinet post.

Four trustees served twelve years each during my tenure:

SARAH VAN HOOSEN JONES, of Rochester, member of a family prominent in human medicine, and herself a successful farm and dairy operator, was a graduate of the Universities of Chicago and Wisconsin but a life-long supporter and generous benefactor of M.S.U. She served as National President of the Association of Trustees of State Universities, and left her family's very substantial estate to M.S.U.

WIN ARMSTRONG, of Niles, was Master of the Michigan State Grange and President of the Michigan and National Association of Rural Letter Carriers. He was particularly effective in dealing with the legislature in M.S.U's behalf.

C. ALLEN HARLAN, of Detroit, an electrical contractor, was especially interested in educational opportunities for worthy students in need of financial assistance.

DON STEVENS, of Lansing, was on the board for twelve years of my tenure and continued as a valuable member of the board after it. He was originally elected as a representative of organized labor and his constant support of the Labor Management Center was particularly helpful in the early stages of M.S.U.'s efforts in labor education.

A Memoir

FRANK MERRIMAN, of Deckerville, another M.S.U. alumnus, was an outstanding Sanilac County farmer, involved in a wide variety of activities concerned with agriculture. He was actively concerned with 4-H Club programs and the Future Farmers Organization. He was an invaluable member of the board for ten years of my tenure. Mr. Merriman was particularly interested in the Michigan Agricultural Conference of which he was one of the original organizers and later its president.

Board members who served for briefer terms include—for eight years—WARREN HUFF, of Plymouth. Mr. Huff came to the board with a wealth of information and background in the federal government and in industry as well as in agriculture. He developed an avid interest in M.S.U., and gave a great deal of his time and energy to it.

For six years—Charles Downing, a farmer of Willis; Ben Halstead, alumnus and lawyer of Petoskey; James Jakway, alumnus, a farm leader and active in the county government of Berrien County; Lavina Masselink, of Big Rapids; Arthur Rouse, of Boyne City; Jan Vanderploeg of Muskegon; and Steve Nisbet, of Fremont.

For five years—Frank Hartman, of Flint, and Clare White, of Bay City.

For four years—Gilbert L. Daane, of Grand Rapids, and Matilda Wilson, of Rochester.

For briefer periods—E. B. More, of Marshall; William Baker, of Mesick; Paul Bagwell, of Detroit; John Pingel, of Detroit; Ken Thompson, of East Lansing; and Blanche Martin, of Lansing.

Among those with six years or less of service to M.S.U. as Trustees, STEVE NISBET should be singled out for particular praise because of his life-long leadership in Michigan educational circles. For many of those years he served as President of the State Board of Education and later as Chairman of the Michigan Constitutional Convocation.

MATILDA WILSON, of Rochester, also took a life-long interest in M.S.U. She later donated Meadowbrook Hall and the 1600 acres of land that surround it, to the university, with two million dollars to pay the cost of building Foundation Hall. This made possible the establishment of Oakland University, first a part of M.S.U. and later given independent status by the board of trustees and the approval of the legislature.

72

LAVINA MASSELINK—Her husband was understudy to Woodbridge N. Ferris, the founder and developer of Ferris Institute, the forerunner of Ferris State College. He succeeded Governor Ferris as the Executive Head of Ferris Institute.

GILBERT L. DAANE was President of the Grand Rapids Savings Bank, well known in state financial circles and also a dedicated trustee.

In addition, reference should be made to the superintendents of public instruction who served ex-officio on the board. They were full members with the right to speak on all matters coming before the board, and in later years, by authority of legal rulings by attorney generals, had full voting privileges.

EUGENE B. ELLIOTT, a twelve-year member, was a constructive and effective trustee. He was an alumnus of M.S.U. and later served for many years as the President of Eastern Michigan University.

LEE M. THURSTON, with a six-year term, also took his responsibility as a trustee seriously. We had offered him an opportunity to join the Michigan State University faculty as dean of the College of Education when he accepted appointment as head of the U.S. Office of Education in Washington, where he served until his early death.

PAUL VOELKER served only for one year from 1934–35. With my appointment on January 1, 1935, he was an ex-officio member with my predecessor for six months and for the first six months of my tenure as secretary.

CLAIR L. TAYLOR served on the board as an ex-officio member from 1954–57. He worked for several years during summer sessions as Director of Summer School and in 1957 joined the M.S.U. faculty as Director of Summer School and Evening College, and Continuing Education.

LYNN S. BARTLETT followed Clair L. Taylor as an ex-officio member of the board from the period of 1958–1964.

Before concluding my remarks on the M.S.U. Board of Trustees, I think it is important to point out the crucial role played by the secretaries of the board in carrying out the work of M.S.U. Karl H. McDonel succeeded me as secretary and served the board and the university for many years. He and his successors—James Miller, later

President of Western Michigan University, and Jack Breslin—were primarily responsible for coordinating the relations of the university with the legislature and with other officers of the state of Michigan. This included the obligation of carrying on the day-to-day work with the legislature appropriations committees. The secretary's office is additionally responsible, in cooperation with the business office, for supervising the building programs and conducting the labor relations activities of the university. It is also responsible for the maintenance of all buildings and grounds of the university, wherever located, which included the internationally recognized herbarium that the M.S.U. campus has become.

Finally, I want to comment on the importance of the university business office in facilitating the work of the university. When I first became president, I inherited the services of C. O. Wilkins, then the treasurer and business officer. Trained as a business accountant, he was conservative in his thinking, close-mouthed and taciturn, and a competent conservator of university resources. To him the details of the university's financial affairs were to be tightly held, limited to only his scrutiny, except during the annual external audit commissioned annually by the trustees.

With the end of the war, our heavy involvement in the self-liquidating building projects, and our rapid growth in enrollment plus spiralling costs, the university developed an urgent need for an active, alert, business management team. There was no alternative but for M.S.U. to completely modernize its business management operations. The Board of Trustees approved of this change, and it became my duty to seek out a competent business officer to install at the university the same type of financial management used by well-managed industrial corporations, with all details relative to the fiscal affairs of the university constantly available to the president and board. I discussed this problem with the best-managed American universities, as well as with banks, industrial firms and other businesses. We knew what we were looking for but so were many other potential employers. After diligent search, we were fortunate to find Philip J. May, who did as much to help to build M.S.U. as any man during my tenure as president. He came as comptroller and was later made vice president for business affairs. May, a native of Pierre, South Dakota, held a degree in business accounting from the University of Minnesota. He played an active part during the war in organizing Army business office procedures in Europe, and at the end of the war he was working for the U.S. Government in the U.S. Reconstruction Corporation.

From the day of his arrival to the date of his departure Mr. May gave the university service of the highest quality. We had, under his management, the best university business office that could be found anywhere in America; he handled our fiscal affairs efficiently, effectively and well. The president or the trustees could call for and get from him all the information they needed about any facet of university business affairs or procedures—often in a few minutes. Under his guidance, M.S.U. funds were always carefully and prudently collected, handled and expended in accordance with the budget and the policies of the university as agreed by the trustees.

An effective administrator of financial affairs does not often win popularity awards. Too often, he has to say no to requests for funds or for relaxations of rules and regulations. Unfortunately two or three trustees became disenchanted with Phil May. In later years, they persistently and often maliciously were publicly critical of him, so that in the end he was hounded out of the university and eventually requested an early retirement. I should like to take this opportunity to repeat what I said years ago to one of the trustees who was a leading critic of Mr. May—that by their tactics, they deprived the university of one of its most able and faithful servants, much to its disservice.

I should also like to single out for approval and gratitude the valuable assistance rendered to the president, the board of trustees and the university by the succession of able legal advisors and external counselors—Ed Shields, until his death, followed by Byron L. Ballard through his lifetime; then former Governor Kim Sigler, until his fatal airplane crash; and then Kim Sigler's assistant, Leland Carr, the son of the late Judge Carr, for many years a Justice of the Michigan Supreme Court.

Few people beyond the central administration of the university realize the demanding and onerous nature of the services required by the university from this important office. The legal officer not only must deal with the numerous lawsuits filed against the university, but he must consult almost daily with the administration to keep the university out of trouble.

You gained the reputation, deserved or not, of being a master lobbyist who could wind the legislature around your finger. Some of us know the difficulties you encountered with the legislature and the budget officer over the years. What comments have you to make on your experiences in the state capitol?

To be thought of as a master lobbyist who could wind the legislature around my finger is an interesting reputation to have. It is not founded in fact, but nonetheless I always felt that I had good relations with the legislature on both sides of the aisle. I made it a point from the beginning to deal with legislators as individuals. I regarded all of them as equal; each one had a vote and each was entitled to equal attention, interest and courteous treatment.

When I was the secretary of the board of trustees, I spent a great deal of time in the capitol. I needed to. The fortunes of Michigan State in the legislature were at low ebb, and one of the first assignments given me by President Shaw was to improve the status of the university with the capitol. I found out quickly that it was not a good idea to try to compete with the lobbyists in Lansing for the attention of members of the legislature. It was much more effective to deal with them in their home districts. I made it a point to travel the state and to visit with them at home, at their places of business, on their farms, or wherever it was convenient. If they wanted me to come, I would show up in the community to meet and talk with them. If they seemed to appreciate it, we followed it up. If they did not seem to welcome it, I did not push things beyond showing up once or twice in a courteous way and then leaving things as I thought the legislator wanted them left.

After I became president of Michigan State University, I took a different stance entirely. I did not go to the capitol unless I was invited. I sometimes sought invitations from the governor or other state officials, and I always offered to visit them in their offices rather than suggesting that they visit me. But I did not enter the houses of the legislature when they were in session, unless I was specifically invited to do so in some appropriate capacity at a committee meeting or hearing. It demeaned the university, I thought, if the president appeared in the capitol in the role of a lobbyist. That does not mean that I did not work constantly at improving our relations with the legislature. I was always concerned with that and I tried not only to be courteous and friendly, but to interest the members of the legislature in the welfare of Michigan State.

What comments do I have to make on my experience in the state capitol? From my point of view, my relationships with most of the legislators were generally friendly and constructive. With all of the governors and the other state officials they were consistently excellent. I cooperated with them in every possible way, going half way or more in dealing with them whenever the university was involved. I tried to answer all questions honestly, completely, and promptly, and always in a friendly fashion. Of course, there were some legislators I liked better than others and, obviously, there were some who liked me better or less well. I made some mistakes and I hope I learned from them.

Now, coming back to the campus, you have always prided yourself as an administrator; what was your general principle of administration: Did you modify it over the years, and if so how?

First, I am not sure that I ever prided myself as an administrator. I think the record indicates that such success as I have had probably resulted, in part at least, from good fortune, hard work, and perhaps some skill. I think that was true of my experience at Michigan State University; I am certain that it was true in the twelve years I was chairman of the United States Commission on Civil Rights. It was equally true of my term as Assistant Secretary of the Department of Defense for Manpower in the Pentagon where I had general supervision of some five million men in the armed services and about three million more blue collar workers in the Defense Department. I believe it was also true of whatever success I had as the administrator of the

United States Agency of International Development for four and one
half years; and equally true of such success as I have had the last four
years working for the United Nations in planning the World Food
Conference held in Rome in November 1974, and since as Executive
Director of the United Nations Food Council. However, I do not feel
it is appropriate for me to discuss my success or lack of it as an
administrator. I would prefer to change the question and make it read:
What were the general principles you followed in your administration
of M.S.U.?

I realized early that if a person's accomplishments are limited to
what he can do only through his own efforts, they will not be large.
In an organization the size of Michigan State when I first became
president in 1941, or as large as it became until I retired in March, 1969,
it seemed absolutely essential that to be successful the university
needed to be staffed by a great number of competent—and more than
competent—people who were willing to work hard in the university's
best interests. It was also essential that they all possess a clear understanding of what the role of the university was, and what its aims
were; and that they be kept constantly aware of any changes in direction, attitude or emphasis.

I do not want to give the impression that in the beginning we had
carefully formulated, specific administrative procedures to be followed to the letter. My attitude toward administration has always
been to learn all that I can about whatever it was that I was trying
to do and then listen to everybody who could tell me something that
might help me do it. This does not mean that I would necessarily
follow their advice or that I would always agree with what they told
me. Rather, I thought that before making a decision I should have all
the facts I could gather from every source, particularly from those
who in my opinion knew what they were talking about.

I quickly learned that it is difficult to achieve an objective unless
it is clearly defined. If one knows *what* it is that he is trying to achieve,
he may be able to do it. But if he is not certain what it is that he wants
to do, there is little likelihood that he will ever accomplish much of
anything significant. To illustrate the point, let us suppose that the
objective is to reach the upper northwest corner of this room. We
would agree that there are many ways to get there. The straight line

is always the shortest path, but sometimes for a variety of reasons—
perhaps involving personality, finances, degree of difficulty, or whatever—we may find that a straight line is not the best way. We can go
up in the attic and come down from another direction and get there.
Or we could go down in the basement and climb the steps or jump
out the window and come in another window or something else and
still get there. But the main point is to always remember where we
are trying to go or what it is we want to do, and try to get there
however we can. I do not mean by hook or crook. We have to fulfill
our aims honestly and honorably. Certainly in an institution like a
university, we have to act always with complete integrity and complete openness. In my experience, I found that if critics ask questions
and demand answers, it is better to tell them the truth from the
beginning, even when one would rather not answer at all.

One of the critical differences, it seems to me, between those who
succeed in life and those who do not is the difference between the
person who sets himself a modest goal, achieves it, and relaxes in the
satisfaction of his accomplishment. On the other hand, the person
who makes a mark in the world is the one who, as he approaches one
goal, already has established another one beyond it, one much harder
to reach. When he gets near that one, there is one beyond that and
still another one as his goals become more difficult to gain.

An effective administrator soon learns that the greatest congestion
is near the bottom of the ladder; the higher one gets on it the more
rare real competence becomes. The most difficult resource to acquire
is adequate human ability, particularly the kind possessed by people
who continue to grow and not by those who with a little success puff
up and sit still with a self-satisfied look. I was fortunate in my early
years in being associated, on boards of directors and through personal
friendship, with successful people in top management positions in
corporations, banks and other large institutions, as well as in the
federal government. I concluded that one of the secrets of success in
the administration of a large organization is one's ability to surround
himself with bright, able people. The more successful corporations or
institutions, I noticed, always had a large reservoir of young persons
being trained for higher responsibilities.

One could always find in the university young, industrious, vigorous, and able people, and as vacancies occurred at the management level I could select from within our own organizations those who might be able to do the job well. After a few unhappy instances when we relied heavily on the recommendations of presidents of other universities or others, we found that we had people of our own who could have done as well and often much better. As a result, we began to look first at our own staff to make certain that we did not have to go outside to recruit. To put it another way, if an administrator does not watch himself, he finds himself comparing the flowery recommendations provided for him by other people with the shortcomings of those on his own staff, and he ends up comparing the strengths of the unknown with the often unimportant weaknesses of the known. My policy was, if reasonably comparable candidates from outside and inside were being considered, to give first consideration to our own. I was always looking over the whole university for bright young men or women, no matter what their posts might be, who seemed to do very well at whatever their assignment. And if they were well trained, well educated, and got along well with their colleagues, I found other opportunities for them to develop their full potential.

A person kept at the same job too long, particularly if he or she is young, frequently loses enthusiasm and the ability to grow. Our basic policy was to move promising bright young persons from one position to another, each time with greater responsibilities, and to keep moving them whenever there was a chance to do so. There were always several people in the university who had demonstrated a potential expertise beyond what their present job demanded. That is one reason why so many of our faculty and staff went on to become presidents, deans, or administrators at other universities, or left for important positions in business corporations. We always recognized that a university is in the business of education—while one hates to see able people leave, yet that is a part of the function of a university.

The key sentence in the question is the last one—"Did you modify your method of administration over the years, and if so, how?" Yes, I modified it. I always modified everything. I never stood still very long at any time in my life, and I hope that I never do. I have never been much interested in the past except as one may avoid mistakes by not repeating them. To me, tomorrow is the important day, not yesterday. Tomorrow, today will be yesterday, and one cannot live it over again. I never learned much looking backwards, and I never wasted much time wishing that things might have been different.

The basic goal—always, all day, every day—was to make Michigan State University the best university we could with the best staff we could assemble. If we were going to make progress toward that goal, the people working for the university had to *want* to work for Michigan State University. They had to be given the recognition and the visibility and the opportunity for growth that all people, and particularly the best young people, want. Otherwise, they will always be looking over their shoulders for these things elsewhere.

I believed that the university needed the best possible internal communications system, not only up and down but crosswise. We had to have a system in which everybody knew where the university was trying to go and one which provided them with ways to express their opinions. Their suggestions might not be followed, but the rule of the game was that everyone concerned should know all the facts and have a chance to discuss them before an administrative decision was made. In the end, if there was disagreement over important matters, the president would present all sides of the matter to the board of trustees who made the final judgment. Once it was made, we followed it out until we found a better way.

Growth and development at the university forced almost constant changes in the administrative structure. Would you comment on the difficulties inherent in the administration of a dynamic institution like Michigan State?

There were constant changes. Obviously, some caused difficulties; there are always difficulties in every changing and expanding activity. But if there were difficulties, we overcame them, one way or another. If we had not had behind us what was once Michigan Agricultural College and later Michigan State College, we would never have become the Michigan State University I left in 1969.

The question refers to "difficulties inherent in the administration of a dynamic institution like Michigan State." I should say again that as president of M.S.U. I never felt sorry for myself. I enjoyed every day of it. Some days were better than others, of course, but I never lost my enthusiasm for the university or for its potential. I have not thought much about the university for the last nine years, but the time I have spent in recording these memoirs has brought much of it back. I am a little surprised to discover that in spite of the two careers that I have had since I left East Lansing, all of the enthusiasm I ever had for Michigan State is still with me.

This is a broad topic. But will you comment on your continuing relationships with deans, department chairmen, and faculty members, individually and collectively? Does growth necessarily entail greater impersonality in administration? How did you manage to keep so closely in touch with campus sentiment, and to provide such outstanding leadership as the university grew and prospered?

Whether the leadership was "outstanding" is not for me to say. I had generally good relationships with deans, department chairmen, and faculty and staff members, because I always respected them, collectively and individually. Each had a job to perform and we respected their assignments. It was my job as president to encourage them to want to make their college or department, or their own activity, whatever it was, of the highest quality. If that required better staff or better facilities or more money, it was my obligation to help them get it.

And it was always part of our overall objective to enhance—or to help individuals enhance—their own reputations. The better and more successful they were, the better it was for the university. If we could have on the staff tens, or dozens, or hundreds of people who were able and talented, certainly they could do a great deal to make a president look pretty good. If we did not have such people, there was nothing the president could do by himself that could determine what Michigan State University was to become.

Earlier in these memoirs I spoke about how we worked to establish internal communications, and mentioned that we had a breakfast group that met every Monday morning at 7:00. All higher-level administrators were there and we talked about what the university was doing. There were no motions and no votes. We arrived at positions and conclusions by consensus. Every Tuesday morning at 9:00 we had a meeting of the administrative group, which included all deans and principal academic administrators. Those meetings served primarily as a communications medium to disseminate information. We made certain that these meetings did not last long. Breakfast meetings were always over by 8:00 A.M. or shortly thereafter; administrative group meetings might last an hour or a little more than an hour, never more than two hours.

I also tried to get around the campus myself. In the early days that was easy, in later years not so easy. I visited every college occasionally, sometimes when the dean or the department chairman expected me to drop by and often when he did not. However, he knew I was there not to ask unfriendly questions but to see what was going on and to show my interest. My door was always open to any administrator, staff member, student, or anyone else could come into the office. He might have to wait for a while, or he might have to make an appointment for another day, but no one was ever turned away. That also was easy in the early days but later more difficult.

After we reorganized the administrative structure, the provost served as alter ego for the president in all matters that had to do with academic administration. The vice president for business was the key man in that area. The secretary of the university was his counterpart in the political area. If we succeeded, it was because we worked at it, and because we had many good people working for the university.

Does growth necessarily entail greater impersonality in administration?

The answer is no. One should never make administration impersonal. A university deals with human beings. Its aim is to encourage every student to achieve the kind of an education he wants and to encourage him to change his goals if he feels the need to. Nor can a college within a university be impersonal, or a department chairman, since they deal with human beings. Growth makes it more difficult to maintain the personal touch, but it is not impossible. It would not be possible for every one of thirty or forty thousand students to visit the university president and talk about himself or herself, but there must be people in the institution to whom the student *can* talk. Naturally, we did not always manage to keep in touch with everyone we should have, but we worked at it, and I think with some success.

> *You are generally credited with the original decision to build the prestige of Michigan State by growing your own faculty, rather than by recruiting established scholars, teachers, researchers. Are you satisfied with the results you obtained?*

As I said previously, we decided quite early that we were going to have to "grow our own." Since M.S.U. grew rapidly at a time when other universities were growing too, the demand for competent scholars and administrators and other personnel was tremendous. There simply were not that many trained people available. For that matter, M.A.C., M.S.C., and M.S.U. in the early days did not have a great academic reputation. It did not have outstanding facilities or outstanding faculty, nor could it pay competitive salaries.

So we had to find a way to improve. First we looked to the better graduate schools, particularly to those we thought were doing things better than we were. I used to say that if we hired ten bright young people and one or two of them became outstanding scholars or administrators or researchers, we were still ahead in the percentages.

We knew that there was no other way. We recognized that you cannot tell by looking at a frog how far it can jump, or by looking at a person how much he can accomplish. There are some things one can judge in a personal interview, but the most meaningful qualities are not easily ascertained. So the best we could do was to hire good people, give them opportunities to grow, and reward those who did. But we wanted to avoid, somehow, the deadly bureaucracies that most large universities and other large organizations can become. Few stars will rise in any organization which does not provide full recognition for outstanding performance with added pay, promotion, or other kinds of recognition. A bureaucracy which recognizes everybody equally and rewards them equally, sooner or later lowers itself to its least common denominator. We had one important rule; no college or department can be improved unless new personnel are better than those being replaced. If the current staff has the opportunity to veto new candidates, you can expect that in general it will approve only those who are no better than the people already there.

Short range and long range, I am satisfied with our policy. As a result, M.S.U. rapidly became a much better university, and I was surprised and pleased at the speed with which the better universities in this country and abroad recognized it.

Would you record your recollection of the famous campaign to get the name of the college changed to university? Would you agree that the success of that mission was a major turning point in the history of Michigan State University? To illustrate, please cite some of the immediate and long-range benefits gained from the change.

I recall the campaign to change the name of the college very well. First, we intended to make Michigan State a distinguished university, worthy of the name. I think we did so, long before its name was officially changed by the state legislature. The name Michigan Agricultural College became inadequate when the college moved from agriculture into engineering, the applied sciences, veterinary medicine, home economics, liberal arts, etc. Michigan State College of Agriculture and Applied Science was a little better, but in much of the world a college or *collegio* is a high school or secondary school.

We talked about a change in name for many years, and when Michigan State became in fact a full fledged university, we wanted it to be recognized for what it was. I am not going to review in detail how the change was achieved, for many people were involved. I had something to do with the planning and something to do with the maneuvering. Interestingly enough, the University of Michigan's persistent opposition and its administration's political tactics in the legislature made it easier for us to accomplish it. By "administration," I refer only to the University of Michigan from the retirement of President Ruthven to the appointment of President Robbin Fleming. Dr. Alexander Ruthven, who was president of the University of Michigan when I became president of M.S.C., was always a respected colleague. Our academic relationships were pleasant and we became warm personal friends. With the appointment of Robbin Fleming as president of Michigan, relationships between the two institutions returned to the pleasant live-and-let-live status we both enjoyed under the Ruthven administration.

Was the name change a major turning point in Michigan State history?

We knew that saying that Michigan State College was a good university would not make it so, nor would Madison Avenue advertising do it. We had to be a first-class university in fact, with a competent faculty and adequate facilities. We believed we were and that other universities believed it too. That was why we spent so much time and energy establishing ties at every opportunity with the administrators and faculties of the nation's most prestigious institutions. For example, people like Lou Morrill, President of the University of Minnesota, were far more effective than anyone in Michigan could have been in carrying the flag for Michigan State. And it was Lou Morrill and his colleagues—a majority of the presidents of Big Ten members—who got Michigan State into the Western Conference when the University of Chicago dropped out. It was Lou Morrill and other friends among the presidents of the American Association of Universities, which included state and private universities and the Ivy League, who helped us gain admission into the Association of American Universities, despite the University of Michigan's determined opposition. But that is all behind us. M.S.U. is what it is. From this point on it will merit such distinction as its performance deserves.

At about the same time, we were putting a lot of resources and time into celebrating the centennial of the institution.

University Administration

Do you think Michigan State gained good dividends on its investment?

There is not any question but that Michigan State University gained a great deal as a result of its centennial celebration. For several months the interest of the whole state of Michigan was directed toward East Lansing. We scheduled a series of events over these months, including national and international conferences, conventions, meetings, and other activities that effectively demonstrated to the people of Michigan just what had happened at Michigan State in the decade between the end of World War II and the celebration of the centennial in 1955.

In 1855 the Michigan legislature passed the law that created the first agricultural college in the world to offer agricultural courses for college credit. That institution provided the pattern for the national network of land grant colleges and universities that followed from the Morrill Act, sponsored by Senator Justin Morrill of Vermont. The idea was not the result of a sudden inspiration by Senator Morrill. It represented the outcome of long years of agitation by groups in various parts of the country who advocated a new kind of higher education through the creation of what was then referred to as "people's colleges" or "people's universities."

Was the time, effort, energy, and money that went into the M.S.U. centennial in 1955 worth it? Emphatically yes. It marked another step toward gaining recognition for the university from all of the people of Michigan. It was concrete proof that after a century of public support, what began as a small agricultural school in East Lansing had become a high quality, broadly based, complex university.

'Cow college' or 'Moo U' are not used much anymore. Did those epithets bother you when they were so common? Would you hazard an informal guess how we finally buffaloed the derisive critics?

Honestly, I cannot say that I was ever irritated by that kind of talk. For some reason many people associated with the university who had a few contacts with agriculture seemed to think that anything that emphasized agriculture necessarily de-emphasized the rest of the university. To me agriculture has always been a respectable vocation, career, or science. In 1955, many people did not fully recognize, as they do now, how important to the world agriculture really is. The food crisis of 1972–74, in part the result of widespread crop failures in many parts of the world, brought death by starvation for hundreds of thousands of people. Millions more were so badly undernourished that they became vulnerable to all sorts of debilitating and fatal diseases. That crisis led to the World Food Conference and eventually to the U.N. World Food Council, with which I continue to be associated.

The "Moo U" type of humor was muffled, in part, by the fact that Michigan State University recognized that cows—like agriculture itself—are respectable, and that one of the real assets of M.S.U. is a strong and widely respected college of agriculture. Probably of more importance in defusing the jokes was the development of Michigan State into a first-class university in every respect, not just in agriculture. We knew that M.S.U. would have to be a distinguished university for quite a long time before our critics would admit it and the jokes stopped. We also knew that there were some highly respectable universities that continue to maintain their reputations long after they have become less distinguished.

You certainly recall that almost every time a substantial new program was proposed at our university, opposition arose somewhere. Sometimes it was in the academic world outside, sometimes in the legislature. Would you discuss one example of each kind: The Basic College and College of Medicine?

In an earlier part of these memoirs I spoke in some detail about how the Basic College got under way, of the part played by Floyd Reeves in encouraging its establishment, and of the appointment of a campus-wide committee in general education under the chairmanship of Howard Rather of the College of Agriculture. The Basic

88

College grew out of studies made during the war when faculty and administration had free time to think about the kind of education that Michigan State College offered as we moved into the war and what might be offered after it. As part of these studies we looked not only at our own programs but those of other comparable institutions around the country—the Big Ten, other state universities, and several of the better private universities, including the Ivy League.

The free elective system, which had been popular for some decades, made it possible for students to earn college degrees and know a great deal about very little, sometimes with little or no understanding of much of what every person who calls himself educated should know. Many of our prospective students, we knew, would come from families in which they were the first members ever to be exposed to higher education. Most of our students would come from Michigan; some of them would be from families who had been in the United States for several generations, but a great many would be the sons and daughters of immigrant or second generation immigrant families.

The high schools in Michigan and other states were not uniformly good. Some did a good job of preparing students for college or university, some did not. Many of the best urban high schools tended to separate students in the early years of high school into those who were probably college-bound, and those who were probably not. Each had different needs and different educational requirements. These and a wide array of other relevant matters were under consideration.

The most significant decision to come out of those studies was that the basic college program was to be a core program of courses required of *all* students. It was recognized that many general education programs—like the good one at Harvard University—were available to students who were alert enough to decide as freshmen that they wanted them. But such programs were utterly meaningless to students who were not enrolled in them. One of our early decisions was that M.S.C.'s basic program would require these courses of all of our students, whether they came intending to major in agriculture, or engineering, or home economics, or one of the sciences, or teaching or business, or whatever.

Once we made that decision, various committees set out to determine what ought to be the components of a general education program. Everyone agreed that no person should consider himself educated unless he had acquired reasonable fluency in his own language. And that meant not only an ability to speak it, but to read it, write it, and understand it. After reviewing courses in English composition and literature offered at M.S.C. and elsewhere, we believed that many of them missed most of these objectives. We decided, therefore, that there should be a comprehensive course in communications required of all students except those who could demonstrate that they had already acquired the necessary skills in reading, writing, and speaking English. All members of the faculty—not just English teachers—should be encouraged to emphasize communication skills in their courses.

It seemed to us also that another component of our program ought to recognize that human beings are biological organisms, living in a biological world. Every person who called himself educated should have some understanding of the biological sciences, some conception of the independence of human beings on the sun for all energy, and some knowledge of life processes in plants, animals, and human beings. These should be included among the objectives of a comprehensive course in biological science. We believed also that there should be similar courses in the social sciences, in the history of civilization, in the physical sciences, and a course in the appreciation of art, music, dramatics and literature. The aim of the entire program was to make it possible for all students to gain some understanding of themselves and of the world, for a full and satisfactory life.

We had to design all of these courses on our own; there was nothing like them elsewhere to be copied. This was a sizable undertaking, to say the least. Our staff visited other general education programs around the country and and then developed our own. The new courses were discussed by all colleges and departments for many months; everyone was encouraged to make suggestions, additions, or deletions.

The Michigan State College faculty voted unanimously to make the Basic College the educational foundation of the postwar university. The university was growing not only in stature, but in competence and confidence. We were making our own decisions as to what constituted university education. The days were over when the M.S.U. faculty would look to Ann Arbor or to Cambridge, or to Berkeley or anywhere else for precedents. There were criticisms, of course. Robert Maynard Hutchins at the University of Chicago, for instance, from a few self-appointed experts, tried to derogate this proposed M.S.U. development. But our faculty committees listened to the critics and then went their own way.

As might be expected, we found out almost immediately that we needed to revise our original concepts. So we set out to make the needed improvements. The Basic College (later University College) made a substantial contribution at that time, I believe, toward a general, nationwide reconsideration of the components and objectives of general education. The idea, in fact, was widely copied with many variations. Over the years hundreds of alumni have told me how appreciative they are for the opportunities it gave them to get the breadth of view, the wide-ranging basic knowledge, that went into their education.

Justin Morrill College, James Madison College, and Lyman Briggs College were experiments in a different direction. The tremendous growth of the university in the fifties and early sixties, as in all public universities, led to questions about the place of the individual student in the huge complex of the modern university—which some believed made him or her feel lost or intimidated. After some discussion we created within the university a series of small residential colleges, designed to appeal to students who wanted smaller classes, closer student-faculty contacts, and a small college atmosphere. At the same time they would be full members of the university student body and enjoy all the advantages that a great university has to offer. Justin Morrill, the first of these, opened in 1965 with a broadly based liberal arts curriculum, emphasizing foreign languages and an international dimension. Lyman Briggs, designed for science undergraduates, and James Madison, for social science majors, were established in 1967. Justin Morrill later shifted its emphasis to lifelong education, but Briggs and Madison are still in operation, quite successfully.

The story of the college of medicine is much different from that of the basic college. It seems today that we were always destined to have a medical program, but originally there

*were many points of opposition to be overcome, especially in
the legislature. Would you review the history of that accomplishment?*

This story is too long to record in these memoirs. Michigan State
had provided premedical education to hundreds of students who then
proceeded to medical schools elsewhere. Because of the strength of
our programs in agriculture and related fields, we were training a
great many biological scientists through to the doctorate in all of the
biological sciences. We determined, as I mentioned earlier, that we
would have only one department in each discipline in the university.
As an example, the department of bacteriology would serve the entire
university. It might have joint membership in the colleges of natural
science and veterinary medicine, but there would only be one department of bacteriology. There would be one department of chemistry,
one department of mathematics, one department of English, etc. We
had to work out all sorts of cooperative relationships to make this
work, but it operated successfully and well.

Experts in medical education continually told us that one of the
problems of medical schools was the fact that they were customarily
separated from the rest of the university, with their own departments
in those applied sciences which pertained to human medicine. Thus,
many medical doctors, for example, were being graduated with little
understanding of human nutrition—which was taught in the college
of agriculture and the college of home economics. Many medical
schools, we found, were turning to veterinarians to staff many of their
research departments, since much of medical research used animals,
and the veterinarians knew more about them than M.D.'s did. Also,
Michigan State had trained bachelor degree nurses for a good many
years and had a strong program in collaboration with many of the
better hospitals in the state. Because of the open-mindedness of our
M.S.U. faculty we were repeatedly urged by members of medical
faculties elsewhere to do some pioneering in human medicine. Some
of the foundations, particularly the Kellogg Foundation, encouraged
Michigan State to give serious conderation to introducing a program
in human medicine. The Kellogg Foundation, in fact, provided substantial funding for preliminary studies and helped our cause.

It was certain from the beginning that any interest expressed by Michigan State in human medicine would meet immediate resistance from the medical school and the administration at the University of Michigan. And it did, vehemently, loudly, and politically. Wayne State was encouraged by some of M.S.U.'s critics to believe that somehow or other it would be better for Wayne if there were only two medical schools in Michigan, at Michigan and at Wayne State. As a result, certain people at Wayne State joined with the University of Michigan in opposition.

The opposition enlisted some of the more powerful members of the legislature to resist every suggestion that M.S.U. develop any kind of program in human medicine. On the other hand, the medical profession in Michigan, by and large, joined in supporting us. The state A.M.A. moved its headquarters to East Lansing, with their State Medical Center on Saginaw Road, not far from the university.

It was a wordy and prolonged battle that generated much more heat than light. The faculty of the M.S.U. Veterinary College, particularly Dean Armistead, joined in the recommendation that the M.S.U. program in medicine be a common core program for all preveterinarians, all premedics, and all of those seeking doctorates in the biological sciences. It was a sensible idea, and it finally prevailed. The interest of the osteopathic profession in establishing a scientifically respectable osteopathic medical program in Michigan, and the decision by Michigan State University to include a separate program in osteopathic medicine, also helped substantially in getting the required legislative support.

Dean Andrew Hunt made a great contribution when he left Stanford University to join us as Dean of Human Medicine. Under his leadership, and that of others like him, we eventually established an excellent medical school, with an excellent faculty and facilities.

Thus far, we have not touched, except in passing, on the underlying philosophy of Michigan State, the so-called land grant philosophy. Perhaps you would take a few moments to discuss that philosophy, and how Michigan State developed in keeping with it.

As I said earlier, land grant colleges were established by the Morrill Act passed by the Congress in 1862. It had been introduced earlier in the administration of President Buchanan and passed by the Congress, but then vetoed by him. The whole movement toward public —or "land grant"—colleges and universities was a result of the belief held by an increasing number of people that if America was to realize its full potential there needed to be a new and different emphasis in higher education.

The nation needed, and needed badly, large numbers of people trained to build the roads and bridges and railroads necessary to open up the country. Engineers, technicians, agriculturists and many others with a wide variety of undefined skills would have to be trained to man the industries, shops, stores, and factories that an expanding nation must have. The Morrill Act set aside federal lands for the states and territories, with the understanding that each would be entitled to an allocation of land on the basis of 30,000 acres for each congressional representative and 30,000 acres for each senator. In the northeast, where the federal government did not own much land, the act empowered those states to go out west, select lands in other areas, and grant them to the new land grant institutions. The money from the sale of these lands was to be invested and the interest used in perpetuity to establish and maintain in each state and territory at least one college where the principal object should be training in agriculture and the mechanic arts (which we now call engineering)—including military tactics—and such additional subjects "as are from time to time deemed desirable for the educational improvement of the industrial classes in the various pursuits and professions of life." That was it. The institution in East Lansing was one of the original models for the system. Senator Kinsley S. Bingham of Michigan, a colleague of Senator Morrill's, played a substantial role in helping to sell Morrill's idea to Congress and the President.

With the establishment of these new institutions, the direction of higher education in America changed. Previously American colleges and universities had been patterned largely after British and European examples. Colleges and universities had originally grown out of the seminaries fostered by the Roman Catholic Church and designed for the education of priests and clergy, later including the children of the rich so that they might live lives of genteel idleness. After the Reformation, each religious denomination, concerned with the training of its clergy, established its own seminaries. Many of what started out to be seminaries later became more broadly based colleges and universities.

In the new land grant institutions, there was to be no denying or downgrading of learning, but the emphasis was to be on the *utilization* of learning for the service of people. And for the first time in history, it became respectable to emphasize college courses that would produce more effective farmers, engineers, housewives, or business people, or that would help them earn a living and develop personal philosophies that would make life more satisfying than it might otherwise have been.

Michigan State University, from its inception as the agricultural college of Michigan in 1855 and after its designation in 1862 as the Michigan Land Grant University, remained true to the basic concept of the Morrill Act. It taught agriculture and engineering and home economics and veterinary medicine. It trained scientists and teachers and business men and women, and it taught communications and medicine and all of the other complexities that have since been included in the teaching, research, extension and continuing education programs of the university.

Michigan State always defined its educational mission in broad terms that widened more than ever during the years I was its president. We believed that if there was anything that the university could do that would help people develop their talents for the service of society or for the improvement of their own lives; or anything it could do to promote a better understanding of the world around us; or any way in which it could help its students to develop their own philosophies—that it would do.

This attitude led us at the end of World War II to emphasize our services for returning veterans. We wanted first to make certain that each prospective student had a sincere desire to develop himself; we assumed that every man who had served his country in battle or had offered to do so, was entitled to the best and most open educational opportunity. We were broadminded in admitting veterans and reasonable in giving them time to adjust to peace time academic life. But if we believed any veteran, man or woman, was not seriously interested in an education, or had neither the desire or competence to make satisfactory progress toward it, that student was invited to leave.

In the early years of my administration, we were much more tolerant about admission requirements for students coming directly from high school than we were later on. In later years, practically all young people graduated from high school, but to many high schools a diploma was only a certificate that the person who received it had been enrolled in some kind of educational program for the prescribed number of years. The diploma was no assurance that the graduate had learned much, or that he or she had either the desire or the ability to profit by what M.S.U. offered. As time passed, we had to become much more restrictive in our entrance requirements.

Since M.S.U. was interested in attracting outstanding student prospects from all over the country and the world, we instituted the Honors College in 1956. This program did much to enhance the reputation of Michigan State as a distinguished educational institution. The Honors College did not in any way derogate or denigrate other programs designed for students proceeding in the regular curricula at the average rate. The presence on the campus of numbers of extremely bright students not only did much to raise internal morale, but served notice beyond the campus that the university in East Lansing was indeed a high quality university, one whose graduates could compete effectively with any from the best universities of the world. We are proud of the fact that for years, Michigan State had more National Merit Scholarship winners enrolled in East Lansing than at any other university in America. This drive toward academic excellence did not lessen M.S.U.'s dedication to the basic philosophy of the land grant colleges.

Michigan State University not only adhered faithfully to the Morrill Act concept, but during the years that I was its president, certainly no American university excelled M.S.U. in its effort to maintain and extend the land grant concept of a willingness to offer its services to all who were interested.

Certainly the idea of the university—any university—carrying a responsibility to the public, is now widely accepted and adopted. But some critics still persist; I suppose Robert Maynard Hutchins, for example, remains to be persuaded. Do you recall the derision he leveled at our School of Packaging program, for example?

I remember very well Robert Maynard Hutchins' derisive remarks on this and many other subjects. They greatly disturbed many people, but never troubled me very much for I had tagged Hutchins much earlier as a fraud. He was best described by one of my university president colleagues as a "self-appointed hair shirt for American higher education." I knew Bob Hutchins well and saw him often. At one time he tried to persuade me to join his administrative staff at the University of Chicago. Like many other persons I have known, he created an image for himself of caustic critic, and he persisted in criticizing even when he was wrong. He assumed a posture, and lived with it to the end.

Now to the facts in the matter. The curriculum in packaging was not intended to be compared with a program in the classics or philosophy, nor should it be. But that need not mean that Michigan State or any other university ought not to provide an academic program in packaging to help train those who expect to devote their lives to the development of that industry. Establishing it did not in any way impede or deemphasize any other program at Michigan State. I made no apologies for the program in packaging then and make none now —or for any other practical programs given for university credit, or for a great many more offered in Continuing Education.

I remember particularly a sarcastic article by an author who had a column to fill and did not know how to fill it, in which he attacked the Continuing Education Program in horseshoeing. At the time horses had pretty well disappeared from American farms but the writer did not know that there are now more horses in America used for recreational purposes than there ever were in the days when horses did most of the farm work. So there was a need for persons who could make metal shoes and put them on horses. For years the only training program in America was the one in East Lansing, which was a short term no-credit course. There were always long lists of people waiting to enroll in it, and the tuition charged was only enough to cover the cost of the course. The horseshoeing course met a real practical need, but the writer wanted to imply that such courses ought not to be tolerated on any university campus. I have always believed that there need be no competition between the most scholarly academic program in the university and those designed to help people earn a living or develop their talents—so long as both serve the public interest.

Perhaps this would be a good place to say a few words about the Cooperative Extension Service and the Agricultural Experiment Station, and how they work with the central university in serving the public.

I am glad to speak about Cooperative Extension and the Agricultural Experiment Station because I have the highest regard for both services. I have maintained that high regard from the day I first went to work for Michigan State College as an extension poultryman in Cooperative Extension, where I spent ten years. I learned much from that experience that I will not go into here, but one thing I did learn was a great respect for working people, particularly farmers. I had to deal with people wherever they were, and if that called for a speech standing on a manure spreader or in a hay mow or on a demonstration field, that's where I spoke. I learned that you cannot sell anything—including facts—until you sell yourself first, and that you cannot sell yourself unless you are completely sincere, unless you work hard and respect all those you meet, regardless of their status or role in society.

I am tempted to tell the story of the establishment and development of the Cooperative Extension Service, but other people could do that better than I. Its record stands for itself, and needs no defense by me or anyone else. It has, from the beginning, always operated in the public interest.

That is also true of the Agricultural Experiment Stations. When Congress decided to subsidize agricultural research it decided that there should be an Agricultural Experiment Station in each state—in part subsidized by the federal government—and that it would be located at the land grant college and administered through the agricultural department of that institution. The United States Department of Agriculture would carry on research in its own centers, but the whole system would be coordinated. It has been and the record is good.

A hundred years ago eighty-five percent of all the working people in America were on farms, producing food or fiber or processing what they produced. America is now a complex industrial society with less than four percent of its people engaged in the production and processing of agricultural produce, yet we have the most efficient agriculture in the world. This is due in large part to the work of the great experiment stations and research centers, and to the dissemination of that knowledge to farm people through the Cooperative Extension Service. As Executive Director of the World Food Council of the United Nations, and as one concerned with the problems of producing food for people in the world's poorest and hungriest countries, I can testify that the Cooperative Extension Service, the Agricultural Experiment Stations and other associated research programs in America have not only made life better for Americans, but have made possible great improvement in the quality of life for hundreds of millions of people on every continent.

I am troubled because M.S.U. no longer has earth-bound agriculturalists in its top administration. It is most unfortunate that of eight members of the Board of Trustees there is not a single one who has any real acquaintance with working agriculture, and very few in higher level university administration. This should be a matter of concern to all. If M.S.U. is to maintain the common touch that a university must have to retain public support in the future as in the past, it must keep its feet on the ground and its head out of the clouds, at least part of the time.

You know, of course, that some critics, especially Ralph Nader, denounced the two agencies for ignoring the interest of the general public, and he seemed to see something evil in their efforts to reduce the amount of physical labor required in crop production. How much credence do you place in their accusations?

These allegations are meaningless. Mr. Nader may be an intelligent man, but he does not know what he is talking about when he attacks the extension service or the experiment stations. Let us take an example. The market demand is for tomatoes that can be shipped without bruising. That is the only kind customers will buy and, therefore, it is the only kind farmers can sell. So the experiment stations are called upon to develop tomatoes that look good and ship well and have long shelf life, because that is what their growers and shippers want them to do. It is unfortunate that our agricultural research workers were not more concerned with taste and the qualities that make a tomato more attractive to the people who eat them. The maintenance of flavor and eating quality can be combined with shipping quality, and shelf life, ability to withstand bruising, etc. From that point of view, Mr. Nader's criticisms are helpful. They helped to focus attention on the fact that publicly-supported agricultural research should always be concerned about the interests of the consumers who pay the taxes as well as the interests of the producers or processors or marketers.

As to the statement about "evil in the efforts to reduce the amount of physical labor required in crop production," the answer to that is if we do not take "stoop labor" out of agricultural production, we will not have much production. American workers are no longer willing to do the kind of labor needed for the production and harvesting of food and other crops. As a result, American farmers have had to emphasize mechanized agriculture, to make large investments in machines to supplant the stoop labor no longer available. Certainly, no one should encourage illegal immigrants from Mexico or elsewhere to serve as serfs moving from one place to another during harvest season, living under bad conditions and with too low income. Developments in recent years that have discouraged that situation are all in the public interest.

Nor have we touched more than briefly on our program of Continuing Education, which has had its difficulties too. Perhaps you would like to recall President Kenyon Butterfield's efforts in that area, and his failures.

University Administration

President Butterfield was a respected teacher and president of what is now the University of Massachusetts, then known as Massachusetts Agricultural College. He was a graduate of the Michigan Agricultural College, where his father was Ira Butterfield, long-time secretary of the board. Mr. Butterfield was persuaded to return to M.A.C. to become its president, bringing with him his interest in what was called continuing educaton. That basic program was and is part of the philosophy of the Country Life Association in which Butterfield had been active, both in the United States and abroad. The more conservative faculty members on the M.A.C. campus who did not agree with him criticized him as too liberal, too highbrow, too far from the soil, and that sort of thing. Some members of the staff of the institution encouraged farm groups to criticize him, as well.

As a result, the State Board of Agriculture at that time, I think most unfortunately, decided while President Butterfield was traveling in Europe to discharge him without notice. The newspaper stories implied that he was discharged because he ran the institution into debt, that he was not business-like in his handling of funds, etc. I have always believed that he should not have been fired without an opportunity to defend himself against whatever charges were made. There was a long gap between President Butterfield's departure and the time I became president of Michigan State University, but even in the early years of my presidency, I ran across people all over the country who felt he had been unfairly treated, and I agree.

President Butterfield was a strong advocate of continuing education. He brought Dean John Phelan with him from Amherst to head up such a program and made him, in essence, what we would now call provost of the university. This was not popular with some members of the M.A.C. faculty, and as a result, continuing education, informal education, and off-campus education were soundly condemned by many of them. With the departure of Butterfield, the program was deemphasized and eventually discontinued. But the basic idea was sound. The land grant university of Michigan should always be alert to helping the working people of the state learn whatever they need to know to be more effective in their work, to give them a better understanding of our society, or a better knowledge of the world they live in.

At M.S.U. we were convinced that we needed to expand off-campus education of two kinds: one, credit courses for those who looked toward degrees; and two, equal or greater emphasis on noncredit programs for persons not seeking degrees. Michigan State did not have sufficient resources to effectuate either fully. I remember very well the months and years in which we tried to find ways to develop these programs in what we called, as Butterfield and Phelan did, "continuing education."

Floyd Reeves, when he came from the University of Chicago, brought a good many ideas with him. One thing that made him particularly useful was his interest in this broad concept of noncredit education for all kinds of people. I mention him here because I spent a good deal of time talking with him, trying to devise a program with a content and a character that might make it attractive to the Kellogg Foundation.

We finally developed something we thought was pretty good. I remember very well the day I first went to Battle Creek to talk to the Kellogg Foundation and to ask Dr. Emory Morris, who was then its president, to provide a substantial grant to build the continuing education center (now known as the Kellogg Center) and to finance the operations of the program for its first few years. A great deal rested on the outcome of that visit, and about all I had going for me was the fact that I had come to know W. K. Kellogg pretty well. After he became blind he kept his great interest in Arabian horses and in agriculture and had developed his farm near Augusta, which eventually became a part of the M.S.U. Kellogg Bird Sanctuary and Farm.

Fortunately, the foundation gave us the grant and we started on a program that was almost immediately copied by other land grant universities. The M.S.U. Kellogg Center and the Kellogg program at Michigan State were both widely imitated, not only by public universities, but by private institutions all over America. The Kellogg Foundation subsequently financed several of them.

M.S.U. emphasized continuing education because we believed in it. We still believe in it. I have said over and over again in my work at the World Food Council that only *people* are important—this is as true in the poorest countries of the world as it is in the United States. Anything that a public or private university can do to provide opportunities for people at the bottom of society's ladder to help them to climb a bit further up is appropriate for that university to do.

How were your splendid relationships with the people at Kellogg Foundation established? Do you count the success of the continuing education program among your major achievements as president?

I believe I have already given most of the answer to this question when I spoke of our long relationships with the Kellogg Foundation that began with my first acquaintance with Mr. W. K. Kellogg. Before I knew him, he was a personal friend of President Robert Shaw, my predecessor.

One of the assignments given to me by Mr. Shaw was to visit Mr. Kellogg at least once each year. Mr. Kellogg was blind at that time and lived in his home on Gull Lake, now owned by Michigan State University. My second or third visit to W. K. Kellogg surprised me. I had not thought much about the last visit until I started to travel to Battle Creek and I was amazed to have Mr. Kellogg start his conversation exactly where we ended our previous one many months before. I later learned that his secretary made a record of what was discussed and then, before I came, reviewed it with him. I soon learned that you never went to talk to Mr. Kellogg unless you had thought through what you were going to talk about.

Later, I came to know Emory Morris, the president of the Kellogg Foundation, very well. Dr. Morris was one of my closest and best friends. I always enjoyed visiting and working with him. Years after our first meeting, when I was asked by the Foreign Relations Committee of the U. S. Senate to conduct a study of development assistance in the Asian countries in which America had spent the most money —Japan, Taiwan, the Philippines and Korea—I took Dr. Morris with me as one of the members of the team.

We had an understanding with Dr. Morris and the Kellogg Foundation that whenever the University had a good project that we had reviewed thoroughly, the foundation would examine it carefully, which meant that in most instances they would finance it. This made it possible for Michigan State University to do many things that it would not have been able to do otherwise.

And I do, of course, count the success of the program of continuing education as one of our major achievements and I am proud to have played a part in it.

I am sure you are well aware that the role of the president as leader has been deflated at most universities, and that students and faculty members have had more and more power of influence, if not decision, conceded to them. Now, a difficult question: Would you have been able to succeed as you did, had you encountered conditions such as they are today when you became president of Michigan State in 1941? Do you think this near revolution against central control has been good or bad for higher education?

I do not agree with the reference to "central control." I pointed out earlier, when I discussed university administration, that we tried always to involve all the appropriate people in making every decision. We listened to everyone who had anything useful to offer. A basic principle of mine was to try to remember how much I learned from critics in the past and how often what I learned prevented what might have been mistakes. I do not think we had "strong central control" at Michigan State. I hope we had strong leadership, not only from the front office, but from everywhere else in the institution.

Now to answer the question, "Do I think that the new so-called administration by faculty committee is good or bad?" I think it is bad. I think it has slowed down change, and I think it will get worse before it gets better. It is a mistake to encourage employees of an institution to think that they have an inherent right to manage it. The board of trustees is elected by the people of Michigan and given by the state constitution the sole and exclusive responsibility to appoint a president for the university. The trustees are the final authority for the management of the university, and it is the responsibility of the board of trustees to protect the public interest. The public interest and the selfish interests of the employees of the university are not always the same—in fact, I think in most instances they are not the same.

If the administrative system of the university is to work success-fully, it is necessary that the board of trustees recognize their role. Their role is to see to it that the university always remembers the purpose of *all* education, the purpose of *public* education, and partic-ularly the educational purpose of Michigan State University.

My answer is, then, that I think that the "near revolution" against central control in the universities has not been good for higher educa-tion.

PART IV
INTERCOLLEGIATE
ATHLETICS

Michigan State has long enjoyed an enviable reputation in intercollegiate athletics, both for the breadth and quality of its program. Your own interest in athletics is no secret, so would you discuss it? First of all, did your interest arise from your own athletic activity as a high school and college student?

I did not participate in high school athletics. I was substantially younger than the average members of my high school class. I lived on a farm some miles from school and either walked or rode a bicycle to school. That meant I had to leave early in the morning to go to school and since I had work to do after the school day was over, I went directly home. I did not participate in any formal athletics in college. I became interested in intercollegiate athletics while I was a student at the University of Michigan in Ann Arbor, due in part to my association with other students who were very much interested in athletics, some of them members of the U. of M. athletic teams.

When I transferred from the University of Michigan Law School to M.A.C. I hoped to complete the requirements for the degree in agriculture in a single college year. I had no time, then, for athletics.

My active interest in athletics at M.A.C. began during the years that I was doing agricultural extension work. I was unmarried and became interested in attending as many football, basketball, baseball games, and other athletic events as possible. Harry Kipke, the new football coach, stimulated a good deal of enthusiasm for M.A.C. athletics. He had been an assistant coach at the U. of M. and since he was not successful at M.A.C. he soon went back to Michigan as head football coach.

There was a growing desire on the part of M.A.C. people to improve the quality of their athletic programs. Jim Crowley, one of the famous Four Horsemen of Notre Dame football, succeeded Harry Kipke. He was a likeable, active and popular person. He and his wife lived in a house on Michigan Avenue in East Lansing on the north side of the street, across from where the Brody dormitories are now located. I came to know Jim Crowley and his wife Helen well and was often entertained in their home. That relationship encouraged me to visit high school athletes in Michigan, particularly in the more remote and rural areas of the state, to try to persuade as many of them as possible to attend Michigan State.

My relationships with Jim Crowley and his assistant coaches, Glenn Carberry, Mike Casteel and later Frank Leahy, developed into substantial personal friendships. I attended all football games at home and away. I particularly remember a night game with Georgetown in Washington for two reasons. We lost the game but Crowley was so favorably impressed by a young Georgetown coach, Frank Leahy, that he later persuaded him to come to East Lansing as one of his assistants.

The team, coaches, and a few others were invited the next day to meet President Hoover in the White House. He came out into what is now the rose garden and shook hands with everybody and said a few words. During the White House visit, when the coaches, the team, and other members of the party were presented to the President, Glenn Carberry, the big rough-hewn line coach, had his gloves on and did not bother to take them off when he shook hands. A picture of him shaking hands with President Hoover with his gloved hand was the source of a good deal of ribbing for Carberry.

In those years, Fordham University in New York, a well publicized football team, was a potent football power. Fordham had aspirations to be the equivalent of the No. 1 team of that time. A game was scheduled with Fordham in New York, and our team, using only twelve men, defeated Fordham to the great surprise of all the experts. After that season was over, Fordham lured Jim Crowley away from Michigan State to New York, where he coached for many years with great success.

Frank Leahy, who later became famous at Notre Dame, wanted to succeed Crowley, but President Shaw thought he was too young and inexperienced. At that time, I did not know President Shaw very well, but I did muster enough courage to suggest that Mr. Leahy had some qualities that ought to be examined and considered. Instead, President Shaw and his advisors chose Charlie Bachman (Charles W. Bachman), who was head football coach at the University of Florida.

I was living in a room on the second floor of the Union Building.

The upper floors had not been completed but there were about a dozen guest rooms that were rented to visiting alumni or others. I rented one of them for several years and whenever I was in East Lansing that was where I lived. When Charlie Bachman came to town as the new football coach, his family remained in Florida until the end of the school year and he and Tom King, the new line coach, lived for a few months in rooms on the same floor of the Union. From this beginning, we became good friends. Later, I played a substantial role in helping Bachman and King attract prospective football players to M.S.C.

In those days we did not talk about "recruiting" students, but we did spend time trying to convince them to come to East Lansing. We had few inducements to offer prospective students except our enthusiastic desire for better teams. We had no scholarship funds, no gifts or blandishments of any economic value. It was the depth of the depression and all that Michigan State could offer was an opportunity for a young man to come to college. If he had no funds or family help, he might be able to borrow enough to pay his tuition and we might be able to help him get a part-time job. During those days, the going rate for student jobs was thirty-five cents per hour.

There was only one dormitory for men on the campus and that was old Wells Hall. It had limited capacity, and most students did not consider it to be a particularly desirable place to live. Those men who could afford living in the fraternities or the rooming houses over in town preferred them to Wells Hall.

During those years, I was one of the organizers of a cooperative boarding club, located in the basement of Wells Hall, where students could get meals at a low cost of about $2.50 a week. Each member worked a certain number of hours per week in the kitchen, helping to prepare the food, serving tables or washing dishes. If the student did not have enough to pay the cost and he came from a farm, he could substitute farm produce, potatoes, eggs, meat or vegetables in lieu of cash. This club was specifically for athletes, but open to all male students who were struggling to stay in school. It was a cheaper way for students to feed themselves than in East Lansing restaurants or boarding houses. Today, of course, there are subsidies for athletes and band players and students of all kinds—subsidies that come with little or no effort on the part of the student, and for that reason are not

III

always fully appreciated. Today, it seems to me boys and girls of high school age take it for granted that they are all entitled not only to scholarships for tuition but expect board and room and spending money as well, without effort on their part.

But to return to the question:

My interest in athletics did not come from participation in athletics myself. It was due to the friendships that I developed over the years, first with Jim Crowley and his assistant coaches, later with Charlie Bachman, Tom King and the coaches of that time, when Michigan State's program had widened from football to basketball and track and other teams. During that period Ralph Young was athletic director. A large man physically, with a large and generous heart, Ralph was interested in all kinds of people. He was never knowingly unkind to anyone, and he was also an effective administrator. I respected Ralph Young as a person and as a friend, as I did John Kobs, Karl Schlademan and a great many others.

Some of the old timers remember that you made places in your own home for several athletes after you became secretary of M.S.C. What led you to do that? Who were some of them?

When I returned to East Lansing as the Secretary of the State Board of Agriculture and Secretary of the College, it seemed desirable to have a house or a home of some kind where I might entertain people, on occasion. I was still unmarried, and I rented a furnished house at 838 Sunset Avenue in East Lansing from a faculty member who was on leave. It did not seem to be sensible for me to live alone in this house, so I invited two students I had persuaded to come to Michigan State to move in, offering them board and room with the understanding that they would keep the furnace going and do some of the housework. One of them was George Packowski, whose father worked on a farm owned and operated by my brothers as a part of their poultry business in Grand Rapids. George Packowski had played football at Grand Rapids Central High School, later graduated in Chemical Engineering from Michigan State and went to work immediately with the Seagram Company in Canada. After an interim period out for U.S. military service during the war, he returned to the Seagram organization and now has an important position in their New York City headquarters.

The second student was Arthur Brandstatter, whom I had also prevailed upon to come to East Lansing. I remember very well visiting him and his family, who operated a grocery store in Ecorse on the Detroit River. Brandstatter had been an outstanding high school player on a football team that did not win many games, but he had the capacity to be an outstanding college player. I remember talking to his father and mother, and later driving down to Ecorse to bring him to East Lansing when he first enrolled as a student, delivering him at Wells Hall along with Milt Lehnhardt from Detroit. The two had not known each other before but they became roommates in Wells Hall. Milt went on to become an architectural engineer for a Detroit firm. Brandstatter majored in police administration and worked first for the Detroit City Police Department, and then returned to East Lansing in a joint role as the head of our M.S.C. police training program and in charge of the East Lansing City Police Department. Over the years, Brandstatter provided the leadership needed to develop an excellent program in police science. After retirement from M.S.U., he is now in charge of a National Police Academy in Georgia operated by the United States Treasury for training police officers for the federal government. After military service, he remained in the United States Army Reserve and eventually retired as a brigadier general.

These were the only two men who lived with me at the house on Sunset Avenue, though, of course, many others were in and out for meals or conversations. At that time I knew a number of athletes. Many were employed by the National Youth Administration in part-time jobs on the campus for thirty-five cents an hour, and they worked hard at it. They put in an hour's effort for every hour's pay.

For many years you attended every Michigan State football game, at home or on the road. How long did you keep the string intact? When did you finally end it?

It is true that for many years I attended all Michigan State football games, home and away. I enjoyed them. I had a personal interest in and relationship with the coaches and with most of the athletes. I was father confessor and informal adviser on all sorts of problems to many Michigan State athletes and other students in those days.

How many years did that continue? I have forgotten, but it was for many years. I ended it after Ripley in his "Believe It or Not" cartoon in the daily newspapers made reference to the fact that John Hannah, President of Michigan State, had attended 120 or more consecutive football games. With that I decided neither I nor M.S. U. needed that kind of publicity.

My interest in athletics gave me an opportunity to know a cross section of students, to know them personally, to know what their problems and concerns were. And out of that I learned much that was useful to me over the years in dealing with student affairs. While I was secretary I was able to do a good deal to reduce the cost of college attendance for impecunious students. The Wells Hall boarding club that I mentioned earlier and other kinds of student aid helped to make it possible for a great many young people to earn enough money to stay in school. And in those depression days it was not easy.

One of the great satisfactions of my life is the fact that some of the closest friends I have are students who were on the Michigan State athletic teams, many of whom have gone on to do interesting and worthwhile things in a great many different fields.

I was interested in all athletics, probably more interested in team sports than in individual sports. There is something about team athletics that requires a degree of dependence on other members of the team, and thus teaches something worthwhile to those involved. It is my impression that one of the shortcomings of formal education is that it fails to generate in young people an appreciation of the fact that, generally speaking, one does not usually accomplish much working only by himself. One must rely on others to do their part. Accomplishing something meaningful and productive, against difficult odds, is often a team effort. That is one bit of learning that every young man or young woman gains from team athletics.

Intercollegiate Athletics

Some of our trustees shared in your interest and were instrumental in hiring Biggie Munn as our football coach in 1947. Would you discuss their interest, and their part in his selection?

When the university sought a football coach to continue Bachman's successful record, we decided to follow the same policy in looking for a coach that we would if we were looking for someone to head the department of mathematics, agricultural engineering, history, or similar post. We knew we were building a different kind of university in East Lansing, and one of the ways we were doing it was to look for the best possible people to fill important positions.

We knew too that we were going to continue our efforts to join the Big Ten. The groundwork for that was already laid. I was personally acquainted with all of the presidents of the Big Ten or Western Conference schools. Long before Chicago left the conference, there was a midwestern consortium of university presidents made up of all of the Big Ten presidents, the president of Michigan State and the president of the University of Kentucky. Those twelve presidents met regularly in Chicago for a full day at least twice a year to talk over the common problems of midwestern universities.

I never missed one of those meetings, and in them I followed the practice that I always followed in new organizations of keeping my eyes and ears open and my mouth shut. I visited all of the Big Ten institutions whenever I was invited to do so or when there was an excuse for me to do so. And if another university president was interested in athletics, I made it a point to encourage our relationship.

In searching for a coach, we compiled a limited list of the ablest prospects we could identify. We came up finally with a list of three persons. The first name on the list was Clarence "Biggie" Munn, who had for many years been line coach at the University of Michigan under Fritz Crisler and was then head coach at Syracuse University. He had an illustrious record. Everyone who knew him spoke well of him. He got along well with young men, high school coaches, and alumni, and he was a grade "A" coach.

The trustees selected a committee of three members of the board to advise me in filling this vacancy. Number one on the list was Munn. Second was Bud Wilkinson, who later became a most successful coach at the University of Oklahoma; and third was Wesley Fesler, who became head coach at Ohio State where he had been a star athlete.

Before I contacted Biggie Munn, I talked to the president of Syracuse University, whom I knew personally, and told him that I was going to make an offer to Munn. I wanted him to know first, since Munn was under contract to him and his university. He responded that he would regret it, but he could not prevent me from making the offer.

I then talked to Munn on the telephone; he was interested and came to Detroit, where we met in the Statler Hotel. Later that day the three-member committee of the Board of Trustees met with us and before the day was over we had hired Biggie Munn and all of his assistant coaches. The assistant coaches who came to East Lansing with him were Forest Evashevski, (later head coach and athletic director at Iowa), Kip Taylor (later head coach at Oregon State), and Duffy Daugherty (later, of course, head coach at M.S.U.). We held the meeting in Detroit so that there would be no leaks that might embarrass Munn or Syracuse. If he accepted the job and came, that would be that. If he did not, we would interview the next man on the list. But, of course, he did.

The trustees who were members of the committee were Clark Brody, the chairman of the board; Forest Akers, then a vice president of the Chrysler Corporation; and Fritz Mueller, then the president-manager of the Mueller Furniture Company in Grand Rapids and later Secretary of Commerce of the United States. All three were alumni, and all were interested in athletics.

Did you and they calculate coldly that improvement in the football program would benefit Michigan State in other ways?

No. We certainly did not. We considered football as part of the total university. We did not foresee that the new athletic program would become as successful as it turned out to be, or as soon. We certainly hoped that the football program would be successful, and that it would be something that all the faculty, students, alumni and friends of the university as well as the public might approve of.

We know now that it worked out that way happily. Would you like to discuss the subsequent developments in detail, giving some examples in both athletic and academic areas?

The answer is self-evident. I have already explained that Michigan State hoped to achieve membership in the Western Conference and we certainly intended to do whatever we could to advance our cause. I had discussed the subject with many of the presidents of the Big Ten universities and had already let it be known that whenever the conference was about to select a successor to replace the University of Chicago, we hoped that Michigan State would receive favorable consideration. In earlier years, well intentioned alumni, sports writers, and many others had made this suggestion at various times. We recognized that Michigan State needed first to convince the majority of the Big Ten universities that it would be an asset to the conference.

Biggie Munn was a successful coach, a good leader, and an effective recruiter of student athletes. He made a favorable impression everywhere, and of first importance he produced good teams. However, successful teams alone did not necessarily mean that Michigan State would be invited to membership in the Big Ten. It had to qualify first as a worthy member of the conference. The institutions that made up the Western Conference were all complex universities, of high quality, respected not only in the middle west but over the nation and the world. Five of the nine were and are land grant universities—Ohio State, Purdue, Illinois, Wisconsin and Minnesota—with strong programs in agriculture, engineering, and home economics. All are highly motivated toward public service and were closely associated with M.S.C. in the coordinated programs of land grant universities.

I mention land grant membership because this meant that five of the institutions already knew a great deal about Michigan State. We had much in common. Our programs in agriculture, agricultural extension, and the agricultural experiment stations brought the presidents and deans and others together in many joint efforts. Michigan State had long been active in the Land Grant Colleges Association, later called the National Association of State Universities. I had been president and chairman of the board of the association and members of our faculty had played important roles in it for many years. That all helped.

It was generally recognized that Michigan State University was undergoing a period of rapid growth, and that the growth was not only in the size but in the quality of its programs. It was also beginning to be acknowledged that Michigan State was an innovative institution, one that did not necessarily follow precedents; that it was reexamining everything it was doing and was trying to work out new ways to accomplish its objectives. All of this helped too. The factors that influenced the Big Ten to accept Michigan State were equally important in assisting us in being accepted into the American Association of Universities, the most prestigious of all of the organizations of American universities. Membership in the Big Ten and membership in the A.A.U. opened the doors of respectability to Michigan State, including the installation of chapters of Phi Beta Kappa, Phi Kappa Phi, and other honorary organizations of academic significance.

As you have explained, one of the major turning points in the university's history was its election to membership in the so-called Big Ten. How did it come about? What difficulties were encountered? How long had the campaign to gain membership been carried on?

The campaign to gain membership in the Big Ten had been going on informally for a number of years before I became president. Our intercollegiate athletic schedules left much to be desired. Our natural rivals in our part of the country, with the exception of Notre Dame, were the Big Ten schools. We played the University of Michigan regularly, but during the war we dropped out of intercollegiate athletics because we had no able-bodied male students on the campus and the military programs we had did not permit participation in intercollegiate athletics. This was not the case at many other universities where military programs permitted and encouraged athletic competition.

We knew from the beginning that there would be no friendly consideration of Michigan State's cause by the Big Ten if the University of Michigan had its way. We anticipated that Ann Arbor would be unfriendly and critical and obstructive, and that is exactly what they were, not only when we hoped to join the Big Ten, but later when we were being considered for membership in the American Association of Universities. But several other universities, particularly the University of Minnesota, helped us a great deal. My close personal friendship with President Lou Morrill of the University of Minnesota played a key role. Lou Morrill had been on the faculty of Ohio State University for many years. I knew him well there, and afterwards when he moved to the presidency of the University of Wyoming. He was active in the affairs of the National Land Grant Colleges Association, and our friendship continued during the years he was president at Minnesota. Minnesota carried the torch for Michigan State. Purdue, Ohio State, Illinois and Wisconsin supported us; the University of Michigan opposed us strenuously and Indiana and Iowa were noncommittal. Northwestern, too, was friendly.

I recall being invited to meet with the conference faculty representatives at Evanston, Illinois. They asked many questions about Michigan State, about our academic policies, our athletic policies, and our future aspirations. It was clear then that serious consideration was being given to the possibility of Big Ten membership. Perhaps I should emphasize that a university does not *apply* for membership in the Western Conference. You hope to be *invited* to join, and that is what happened.

Final action was to be taken on a Sunday afternoon. At that time, I was the senior warden of the vestry of St. Paul's Episcopal Church in Lansing, and that afternoon I was chairman of some event at church. I remember that as I was getting ready for church, I was much more interested in what was happening in Chicago than in what was going to happen at St. Paul's. When the event was over, Dean Lloyd Emmons, who was in Chicago, had word for me that Michigan State had been invited to membership in the Big Ten.

Membership in the Western Conference brought, and continues to bring, many correlative benefits. Will you discuss what they have been and how you view them?

Membership in the Big Ten immediately gave us much more meaningful schedules for our athletic teams. After we resumed athletic competition after the war, the University of Michigan let it be known that there was no assurance that they would reopen their schedule to Michigan State. We knew that we had no alternative but to try to join in a long-term commitment with Notre Dame in football and other sports. We already played Notre Dame in everything but football, where they were so much stronger that we would not have done very well. Also, Notre Dame played universities with much more athletic prestige who drew much larger crowds. M.S.C. had made a firm decision that all of our athletic contracts were to be on a home and home basis. We would not play away unless our opponent would play us in East Lansing, and playing in East Lansing every other year was not financially attractive to Notre Dame. They needed football receipts not only for their athletic program, but to provide funds toward the operating costs of the university.

Harry Kelly, the Governor of Michigan, was an alumnus of Notre Dame. He invited Father Cavanaugh, a native of Owosso and president of Notre Dame, to meet with me at a luncheon in the governor's home in Lansing. At that meeting we agreed that as soon as schedule arrangements could be worked out, we would schedule home and home football games with the University of Notre Dame for an indefinite period. This series with Notre Dame made it financially feasible for us to increase the size of the stadium—eventually to 76,000 people —and meant that we could now compete with schools anywhere, if our football teams were good enough.

Munn's teams were well coached and he was respected by all who knew him. Ralph Young and his entire staff kept our athletic programs on a high plane. Certainly the quality of the university and its athletic programs were main factors in our invitation into the Big Ten. This was an important step forward for Michigan State, not only athletically, but academically.

Intercollegiate Athletics

To become a member of the Big Ten, Michigan State had to adjust some of its eligibility standards. Were the benefits worth the sacrifice?

The answer has to be yes. It was worth doing whatever we had to do. I think the question is intended to bring up the matter of our Jenison Awards.

The Jenison Awards were established in memory of Fred C. Jenison, an alumnus, after whom the Jenison Fieldhouse is named. Mr. Jenison bequeathed his entire estate to Michigan State and named me as the executor, with the understanding that the funds were to be used for the improvement of the university with particular emphasis on athletics. Part of the funds paid for that portion of the construction cost of the fieldhouse not covered by a federal P.W.A. grant, or approximately fifty percent of the total. The completion of Jenison Fieldhouse marked a big step forward. It meant we could convert the former gymnasium to a center for physical education for women, while providing new facilities for physical education, recreation and health for men.

Jenison Awards were made annually to a fixed number of prospective student athletes who had to meet all of the usual requirements for admission required of other students. Recipients had to have graduated in the top third of their high school classes, and to hold their award they had to make a full year's progress toward their degrees each academic year. He had to have at least a "C" average in all of his *academic* subjects. It was not enough to have grades above "C" in physical education and applied courses and grades below "C" in academic subjects, thus averaging out as "C."

If the award holder continued his interest in athletics, but could not compete successfully because of injury or lack of ability, he could not lose the award on either basis. Jenison Awards amounted only to tuition, fees, and the loan of text books. The student was responsible for his own living expenses. At that time, I might add, in the Big Eight and in the Southeast and Southern Conferences, made up largely of state supported institutions, athletic scholarships generally included board, room, tuition, books, laundry and sometimes spending money.

Since the Big Ten objected to our Jenison Awards, we accepted membership in the conference with the understanding that they would be terminated. We did not play a full schedule in the Big Ten until two or three years later, and the Jenison Awards were phased out before then. Actually, the awards represented a less generous and a more sensible athletic scholarship program than was then in effect in the Big Ten. We said so but we agreed to give them up and to follow conference rules. Time demonstrated that we were right. The Big Ten now provides more generous athletic scholarships, and sometimes enforces its rules more loosely than we did at Michigan State in the old days of the Jenison Awards.

In the early years we had a lot of problems with the Big Ten and the National Collegiate Athletic Association. Do you think we were being hazed or harrassed by some of the older members?

I must say I do not know. After we got into the conference, I devoted less attention to the athletic program, which was supervised by a faculty-controlled Athletic Council. Dean Lloyd C. Emmons served both as our first Big Ten representative and as chairman of the Athletic Council. Later, Edgar Harden, Dean and Director of Continuing Education, was our chairman and faculty representative. When he left for private business, Leslie Scott, Professor of Hotel Administration, succeeded him and for the last years that I was the president, the chairman and faculty representative was John Fuzak of the College of Education.

After admission to the Big Ten, we carefully followed conference procedures. The faculty representatives and the Athletic Council were largely responsible for the development of athletic policies, and I know of no instances which led me to believe that Michigan State was being hazed or harrassed by the University of Michigan or anyone else in the Conference. As far as I know, we were treated fairly.

Some of our coaches were occasionally a bit over enthusiastic and consequently embarrassed us, but when that happened I made it clear to all of our athletic officials and coaches that Michigan State was a member of the Big Ten and the N.C.A.A. and we intended to comply with all their rules. So long as I was the president, I reminded the athletic director and the head football coach at least once each year that *all* of our athletic programs must always be in compliance with the rules, and that if I found any violations, there would be a new coach of football or of whatever branch of athletics was involved. I have been unhappy with press reports of some of the recent happenings that have embarrassed Michigan State University—not only its athletic program and its coaches, but its faculty, alumni and friends. The reputation of the university is much too important ever to be jeopardized by the kinds of violations in which apparently some of our people were involved in recent years.

> *You developed a nationwide reputation for advocating higher standards in intercollegiate athletics and as a champion of reform. Would you discuss this? Do you feel that universities have been falling away from these high standards, as in the so-called "shirting" practice?*

A good many years ago the American Council on Education appointed a national committee of ten or twelve university presidents and I was chairman of the group. We were charged with investigating the whole problem of intercollegiate athletics and coming up with recommendations to remedy what needed to be remedied. The so-called Hannah Committee made a comprehensive study and its report was later published. I have not seen a copy of it for many years, but at the time it was regarded as a forthright, well-thought-out report. It is my impression most of its recommendations were eventually put into effect. If my memory is correct, they were that: first, there should be one standard for admissions for all students, including athletes, and athletes should not be granted exceptions; second, there should be one standard of scholarship for all students, and that whatever was required of all students should be required of athletes; third, that all athletes, in order to retain their eligibility, should be required to make one full year's progress toward a degree between athletic seasons. Nothing would be gained by reviewing here how little many of the presidents of universities of that day knew about the athletic departments at their own institutions.

I withdrew from active involvement with athletics, other than as an interested spectator, for the last several years that I was president, not because of lack of personal interest, but because of lack of time. My responsibilities as Chairman of the U.S. Commission on Civil Rights took a large amount of time, and there seemed also to be more important problems at the university that required attention. The responsibility for the control over athletics ordinarily exercised by the president was transferred to the secretary of the university, Jack Breslin.

To conclude this discussion would you give a general statement on the value of athletic competition at the university level, and something of your basic philosophy governing that aspect of amateur athletics.

I have always thought that a sound athletic program was good for a university. It is good for the athletes, if they are full-time, bona fide students who must maintain satisfactory standards of scholarship and performance. Athletics unify a university probably more than any other feature of the institution. They merge the enthusiasm of students, alumni, faculty, friends and supporters of the university, and all to the university's good.

I do not think winning is the only way to maintain that interest and loyalty. A winning team does not make a university a great university, nor does it detract from a great university. The University of Michigan has never suffered from its success in athletics, nor have the indifferent successes of athletic teams at Harvard influenced its quality. The teams need to be representative; they need to win, one hopes, about half of their games and to compete on an even basis with other members of the conference. I was president when we had good football teams and I was president when we had poor football teams, and in spite of the remarks attributed to me in the press, I never found that a winning football team made any substantial difference in the level of support given to the institution by the legislature or alumni or friends.

PART V
OF CAMPUS
ACTIVITIES

Would you expand on the university's relations with news-papers, radio, television, and similar aspects of Michigan State's services, or on other points you wish to discuss?

The Michigan Press Association, made up of the state's weekly newspapers, maintained its state headquarters on our campus. This was a great asset in our dealings with rural communities, and as rapport improved between the weekly press and the Michigan dailies, the association became a much more comprehensive organization. Their annual week-long meetings were held at Michigan State, and over the years a friendly and cooperative relationship developed between the association and the university.

In the early days, the Michigan State Journalism Department was oriented toward training people for weekly papers and small dailies. I found in frequent meetings with the officials of the Michigan Press Association that they were much concerned with radio as potential competition for the press. The appearance of television intensified their concern. Some editors and publishers believed TV news bulletins, for example, might make newspapers unnecessary. Of course, nothing of this sort happened.

In the process of reviewing all our programs at Michigan State, we took a long hard look not only at the Department of Journalism but at the entire field of mass communication. Instead of establishing a program in radio or television, competitive with journalism, we decided to organize a college of communications, or communication arts, to include journalism, television, radio, public speaking, dramatics, and allied subjects. This seemed a radical idea to many of the academics in the field around the country, and it took two or three years to convince the Michigan Press Association, but as it turned out, we were right. The first formally established college of communications arts was the one on the East Lansing campus, and within a few years it was copied all over the country.

Here I pay credit to Gordon Sabine. The first dean of the college, we believed, should come from journalism, in order to forestall criticism from the Michigan press. In our search for the right person, we found that the one man of all those we talked with who seemed to understand what we had in mind was the young Dean of the College of Journalism at the University of Oregon. The University of Oregon had just provided him with a new building and he was well regarded by the Oregon press, but I convinced him to come to East Lansing. He did a good job for us, recruiting a high quality staff and launching the new college on a distinguished path. Gordon Sabine was an innovative fellow, though he sometimes had problems getting along with other strong-minded people.

Later, when the future of the College of Communications Arts seemed assured, we transferred Gordon to a totally different assignment, the recruitment of the best and brightest students for Michigan State. Traditionally, in Michigan, high school advisors urged their better students to attend the University of Michigan. Not that the high schools were averse to sending their students to East Lansing, but since Ann Arbor had a law school, a medical school, and a comprehensive graduate school, it was not surprising that the best students were often directed there. Michigan State had a strong and loyal following in the rural areas and in the small towns, but not in the larger cities.

So Gordon Sabine was asked to apply his talents in the field of recruitment. First, we had to be certain that we actually had the kind of programs that would serve bright city youngsters at least as well as they might be served at Michigan, Harvard, Stanford, or other similar institutions. He did a superb job for Michigan in developing the resources needed to attract Merit Scholars and he introduced a special Honors College to provide the best for them. As a result, we succeeded in attracting more National Merit scholars than any other American university. The Honors College not only raised the level of our educational effort, but raised our aspirations and our confidence. Clearly, too, it contributed much to the success of our graduates in postgraduate and professional schools.

We knew, of course, that there was nothing to be gained in selling ourselves unless we had something worthwhile to sell, or in trying to convince people that we were an outstanding university before we were. We had no alternative but to improve our faculty, our facilities, our salaries, and our library and laboratories, so that we were what we said we were. Image building can be effective only if there is substance behind the image.

One of your major interests in the later years of your presidency was international education and technical assistance and its importance in the world and on the campus. Did this develop from your personal interest in travel? Your position as leader of the land grant college institutions gave you the rare opportunity to exert leadership when President Harry Truman expanded his program for economic aid to the rest of the world. How did this come about and how did Michigan State, itself, get so deeply involved?

I learned as a young man that travel was educational. It certainly has helped me to understand better the people of the world and their aims, attitudes, and aspirations. I always had an interest in international education, which was strongly encouraged by President Truman's appointment of me to the International Development Advisory Board. When President Truman looked at the world, he found that two-thirds of its population lived in what he called "the underdeveloped world." What the future would be like would depend largely on what happened to these underdeveloped countries. He asked Congress to allow him as President of the United States to extend assistance to those countries that wanted to help themselves, so that they could learn how to use their own resources for their own improvement. This was the so-called "Point Four" program, authorized by Congress, which empowered the President to appoint an International Development Advisory Board of twelve citizens. The first chairman of that board was Nelson Rockefeller, Governor of the State of New York and later Vice President of the United States.

At the time of Truman's inauguration, and as soon as Point Four was announced, the Board of the National Association of Land Grant Universities, of which I was then president, authorized me to extend to him the assurance that the land-grant universities would support his program and do whatever they could to make it effective. We spent a good many weeks trying to figure out how to get Point Four off the ground. The details are unimportant, but as a result Michigan State decided that it wanted to play a part in this effort. The first two U.S. Government Development Assistance contracts with universities for programs in agriculture were with Michigan State for a project in Colombia, and with Oklahoma A. & M. for one in Ethiopia.

Michigan State later participated in many such programs around the world, many supported by the Agency for International Development and its predecessors, some financed by American foundations, and some sponsored by other international organizations.

Michigan State University has been severely criticized for its involvement in the affairs of South Vietnam. Knowing what you do now, do you regret our efforts there? How would you have managed them differently?

Hindsight is often better than foresight, but I think if Michigan State University were again placed in a situation such as it was when we first became involved in Vietnam, we would probably react about as we did then.

The university became involved in South Vietnam after John Foster Dulles, the Secretary of State, telephoned me to ask if M.S.U. would assign one of our faculty to accompany the man whom the United States was backing as head of the new independent South Vietnamese government to the Geneva Conference. The man was Ngo Dinh Diem. I answered that we would consider it, and after I learned more about it we authorized the late Wesley Fishel, Professor of our Political Science Department, to accompany Diem to the conference. Mr. Diem had a great deal of confidence in American higher education. Since the American government had been allied with Britain and France and the Netherlands, all colonial powers in Asia, he was a little suspicious of them all.

Later, the U. S. State Department suggested that Michigan State University might apply for a contract to provide advice and help to the new government of South Vietnam. In response, we authorized four faculty members, one in each of the areas in which they were seeking assistance, to make a trip to South Vietnam, look at the situation, and report their recommendations.

When they returned, they recommended that the university proceed with the application. It was understood that the costs would be covered by the United States but that the advice would be given to Mr. Diem and his government. They asked particularly for aid in the area of public administration. All civil servants, down to those at the township level, had been Frenchmen who had returned to France. There were practically no Vietnamese with the experience and skill needed for public administration at all levels. The first priority was the creation of an institution to train civil servants, so our staff in public administration were the first to be involved.

The Vietnam government's second major concern was economics and taxation. Here they wanted our Economics Department and the College of Business to give advice. Third, they needed expert advice on public relations, on how to deal with the press, radio and television. Fourth, since they badly needed well-trained police—a civilian force, not military—they wanted someone from the Department of Police Administration to help train them.

The Board of Trustees authorized the university to undertake the project. In its early phases we thought it was a very successful program. It was not until years later, when the Vietnam War became unpopular and the subject of much criticism by the American press and the American public, that it was alleged that one or more of our employees had apparently been associated with the C.I.A. We never had any evidence that this was true, though it might well have been the case. *Ramparts* magazine, a West Coast publication that thrived on sensational publicity, ran a major feature about the Michigan State Vietnam program. Much of what was written was not true, but the piece caused the university a good deal of embarrassment. We never felt any need for the university to apologize for its participation in the project or for what we tried to do in Vietnam. We learned a good deal from that experience and became much more careful to make certain that we did not allow ourselves again to be put in a position where an outside agency might compromise us.

I think that if Michigan State were to face the same choice again in the same context, it might well agree to assist the U. S. Government as we did then. Having been in Vietnam as the administrator of U.S.A.I.D. several times since leaving M.S.U., and having had contact with the Vietnamese before and after the war, I think, by and large, the Vietnamese who understood the situation were grateful for what the university tried to do for them.

The University of Nigeria project brought deep disappointment for reasons over which the university had no control. Knowing what you do now, did you think the results were worth the effort?

Yes, I think they were worth it. It was a valuable experience for Michigan State, and we can always be proud of the University of Nigeria at Nsukka that was developed under our contract. Much good has come from it, not only in the east region of Nigeria, but in all of Nigeria today.

The Ibo people, who controlled East Nigeria, later became involved in a civil war with the central government in Lagos, and the University in Nsukka was eventually closed throughout the war. Some Nigerians claimed that the university contributed to the war by making the Ibos independent and self-confident, but I have seen no evidence that this is true. At the close of the war, the Ibos resumed their important role in the government and have helped substantially to put the country back together. However, as a reaction to the attitude of the university prior to the war, the Nigerian government brought in a United Kingdom educator to head the University of Nigeria. He transformed it from what was essentially an American land-grant institution into a British tutorial-type institution. Recently, it has changed course again and seems to be a compromise between the British and the American models.

To understand the situation in Nigeria, one needs to know that prior to Nigerian independence Nnamde Azikiwe was the Premier of the East Region of Nigeria. American educated, he had a great enthusiasm for the basic philosophy of the American land-grant schools and came to the United States to ask for help in building such a university. No one in Washington seemed to be interested. Azikiwe returned to Nigeria and persuaded the East Region government to set aside for a university a percentage of the income from palm nut exports until the funds amounted to five million pounds sterling. Then Azikiwe came back to Washington and asked the State Department to identify an American university he might work with in building it. He had heard of Michigan State, so again the State Department called me to ask if we were interested in the project. First I had to look at the map to see where Nigeria was, and then I made a trip to Enugu, the seat of the East Region's government, and drove out with Dr. Azikiwe to look at the site that he had picked in Nsukka.

While I was there I told him that we would help him build his university, but I thought he ought to involve the British too. Since Nigeria had been a British colony, most of the Nigerians in the new government were British-oriented. In my view, if this new university were to succeed, it needed approval by the British-educated Nigerian leaders. The Premier did not particularly like the idea, but he invited the British to participate in the planning.

Michigan State University did a good job in creating the University of Nigeria. Many people were involved in it. Glenn Taggart, now President of Utah State University, and who was then on our faculty, spent time and energy for many years in Nigeria. I had also become acquainted in my work with the United States Commission on Civil Rights with George Johnson, the Dean of the Law School at Howard University. I persuaded him to leave Howard and join the faculty at Michigan State and the Nigerian project, eventually to become the president—or what in the British system is called the vice chancellor —of the university at Nsukka. He served in that post with great distinction, came back to East Lansing, spent some years in the College of Education and is now retired and living in Hawaii.

I make no apologies at all for the establishment of the University of Nigeria, and I think Michigan State University can be proud of it. We had nothing to do with the Ibo War, and since the war we have not had much to do with the University of Nigeria.

There were many great and acknowledged successes to the credit of M.S.U. in its overseas projects. In all fairness, would you summarize the major ones and discuss them.

It has been almost nine years since I left the presidency, and to answer the question I would have to look over a complete list of university projects and comment on some of the good ones and on some of those which were less successful. In general, I think that over the years Michigan State did well. Many of our projects were outstanding. One of the best was the establishment of the Getulio Vargas Institute in São Paulo, Brazil, under a contract with our College of Business. Brazil had no colleges of business at the time. Brazilian universities, like most Latin American universities, emphasized scholarship for its own sake and had little interest in dealing with practical problems.

In ten years the College of Business developed in São Paulo a grade "A" College of Business, staffed with Brazilians who did their graduate work in the United States. This excellent institution has been responsible for training a substantial fraction of the middle management of the great industrial complex that has developed in the São Paulo region in the last fifteen or twenty years. The success of Vargas Foundation School made colleges of business administration so popular in that country that most leading universities in Brazil now have business programs of their own. At the end of ten years, Michigan State completed its contract, but the Vargas Foundation continues to be an excellent school, proud of its association with Michigan State University.

Another very successful project of a different kind was the Rural Development Academy in Comilla, East Pakistan, (now Bangladesh) financed by the Ford Foundation. Farms are small in Bangladesh; averaging from one-half acre to two or three acres, with very few of five to ten acres. Two and one-half acres is a hectare, and a one hectare farm is regarded as a pretty good-sized farm. The institution at Comilla is one of the best of its kind in the world, largely because of the leadership of its first director, Akther Hamid Khan. I visited it last in December, 1977, and was much impressed with its accomplishments.

Many other overseas programs in agriculture and in education deserve mention. One of the early ones was the building of the University of Ryuykus in Okinawa, where Michigan State helped to establish a Japanese-style university for a territory that was eventually returned to Japan. Michigan State's Taiwan project made substantial contributions to agricultural development there, while the College of Education has supervised some distinctly successful projects in Thailand and in Turkey. The College of Business has had productive programs in Turkey and there have been others in Indonesia, Argentina, Korea, Iran and elsewhere.

It was good for Michigan State University to be involved in these ventures—good for the faculty, the student body, and for the countries where they worked. Through them, Michigan State students and faculty found by experience that what happens in far away places is important to what happens here.

After your years of experience at M.S.U. and your subsequent experiences with A.I.D. in Washington, what is your current thinking with respect to the role of American universities in the foreign field?

American universities have a real obligation to provide their students, particularly those who will never leave the United States, with a much better understanding than they now have of the true nature of the world. After almost four years working within the United Nations, and after nearly a lifetime in higher education, I find our universities and colleges sadly deficient in equipping Americans to adequately understand the world of which it is a part.

If there is to be a peaceful world, a world safe for our grandchildren, then the United States must play a main role in helping to make it so. I believe we can, if we try, create a future world in which all people, of all religions, races, and political beliefs, may live safe, productive, and fruitful lives. People everywhere would like to be assured that they will always be treated as human beings, with dignity and respect. Millions of them on every continent would trade everything they have or ever hope to have for an opportunity to live as American citizens.

My current concern is how the world is going to feed its hungry for the next fifteen or twenty years, particularly the poorest people in the poorest countries. No human right is more important than the right to have enough to eat, so that children brought into the world may grow into the potential God intended they should have. Hungry, starving people are ungovernable and unmanageable. There is no justification for permitting millions upon millions of starving and grossly malnourished people to live into tomorrow's world. Michigan State University and all other universities in America should accept responsibility for an attempt to find a solution for this, our century's primary problem.

Long before you resigned from the presidency, you had established a national and international reputation for leadership in higher education, in academic affairs as well as in administration. The latter can be more readily understood than your leadership in academic affairs, where you had far less experience and no formal educational training. How do you account for that?

I am not sure that what the question says about my reputation for leadership in higher education is true, but I appreciate the intent.

The question leaves the impression that the only way one acquires an education is through taking courses on a college campus and earning degrees. I do not believe that. I never have believed it. Certainly an education is most easily acquired by going to school, taking courses, and working in classrooms and laboratories and libraries. However, I have known many men and women who have gone through the entire system of formal education, including the doctorate, and still lack much of what I think should be expected of well-educated people. On the other hand, I have known a substantial number of well-educated men and women who had little formal schooling. They moved through life with their eyes and ears open, asking questions, reading widely, observing keenly, and they became very well educated indeed.

Education means different things to different people, of course, but whatever it is, it is much more than the accumulation of knowledge. To be well educated one must be competent in his own language; one must be able to read it and write it and speak it with reasonable fluency. One must have an understanding of the biological world of which we are all a part, so that he can comprehend it and appreciate its order and perfection. One must also have more than a superficial understanding of human beings and how to get along with them, some perception of why people behave as they do, and of their hopes and aspirations. An education also, I believe, should help one to understand himself and to develop a philosophy for his own personal life, one that makes it meaningful and satisfying. These things, it seems to me, are ingredients in what makes up an education.

What is the objective of this thing we call an education? How is it defined? How does one achieve it? Part of it we find in classrooms and laboratories and libraries. Part of it is learning how to live with other people and how to understand them. Part of it derives from the development of an insatiable curiosity, a desire to know about everything and to get all the facts—not just those that defend or support what you think or agree with or what you would like to believe, but *all* the facts, pro and con and those in the middle.

One steady purpose in all of my life has been to try to do everything that I undertake as well as it is possible for me to do it. That means understanding what I am trying to do, and changing my objectives as facts, or situations, or accomplishments change. I have watched many people with limited aspirations who, as they approach success, relax and say to themselves, "I have arrived. I have achieved what I sought. I have a good job, a good salary, a nice house, a family." Then they center their energy and enthusiasm on the golf course, or the bridge game, or travel, or gourmet dining, or on something else not very important.

So far as administration goes, I never took a course in it, but if I had some success as an administrator, it may have been because I tried to figure out how to involve as many able and enthusiastic people as I could in helping the institution achieve its goals. I believe, too, that goals must change as situations change. If we succeed at one level, we must seek success at the next one higher.

Nothing is more important to a university than the quality of its on-campus educational programs. If one is given leadership of an institution in which the academic program is, by all odds, the most important part of it, one needs to know and understand all there is to know about its academic life. One need not be an expert in all of the academic disciplines, but an administrator needs to learn enough about them so that he understands their languages and attitudes.

I learned a good deal about administration from many people I had the good fortune to know. I had an opportunity to spend fairly lengthy periods of time with many national and international leaders in business, government education, and other fields. I had the opportunity to know personally all of the presidents of our country from Herbert Hoover through Gerald Ford. I also learned a great deal from some of the labor leaders I worked with, from Walter Reuther, Jimmy Hoffa, and particularly from George Meany. Naming these people does not mean that I always agreed with them. Many of them I did not agree with at all, but I learned a lot by trying to see what made them tick. That is true of the governors of Michigan, all of whom I have known personally, beginning with Alexander Groesbeck. I learned a good deal, too, from my contacts over many years with most of the leaders of American higher education, and with those in the national field of Civil Rights.

In recruiting personnel for Michigan State, in my experiences with the Department of Defense, in A.I.D., in the work of the Commission on Civil Rights, and in more recent years with the United Nations, I never found that there was a close correlation between the courses one took in college and what one was able to do in later life. Formal education may supply one with information that helps you through the first door to the first job, but from that point on your future is largely in your own hands, dependent upon your ability to do what is expected of you and what you expect of yourself. The ability to understand people and to get along with them is very important—and that includes tolerance for all people and all points of view. One cannot deal intelligently with people unless one understands what makes them think as they do.

I should warn the reader not to misconstrue my remarks about the relative values of formal education and broad life experience. Excellence lies at the heart of one's personal education as it lies at the heart of a university, and I would never denigrate the value of academic training. I never earned a Doctor's degree. As a young man, I did not know that I was to spend most of my life in educational administration until I reached the point in my career where an earned doctorate would have made me no better and no worse at my job. I never apologized for it, but if I were to live my life over I should certainly try to earn a doctorate early in life. I called this to the attention of the State Board of Agriculture when they first raised the possibility that I might be offered the presidency of Michigan State, pointing out that in the eyes of some academics my lack of an earned Ph.D. degree would be viewed as a serious deficiency. The board brushed it aside. I was awarded honorary doctorates by many respectable universities —more than thirty of them, including several outside the United States. I was always grateful for this generous recognition but never regarded all of them put together as a substitute for an earned doctorate.

PART VI
CONCLUSION

The last in the series of questions is:

Conclusion: Anything else?

Only this:

I am exceedingly grateful:

(a) for having had the good fortune to have been born and raised in the State of Michigan,

(b) for having become associated with Michigan State University,

(c) for having had the opportunity to come in contact with many of the leaders of the State of Michigan and with leaders of nations all over the world.

There are few people who have had an opportunity to live a more interesting life than I. It all was made possible as a result of my role at Michigan State University. For that I am grateful to the university and the people there who helped make it possible.